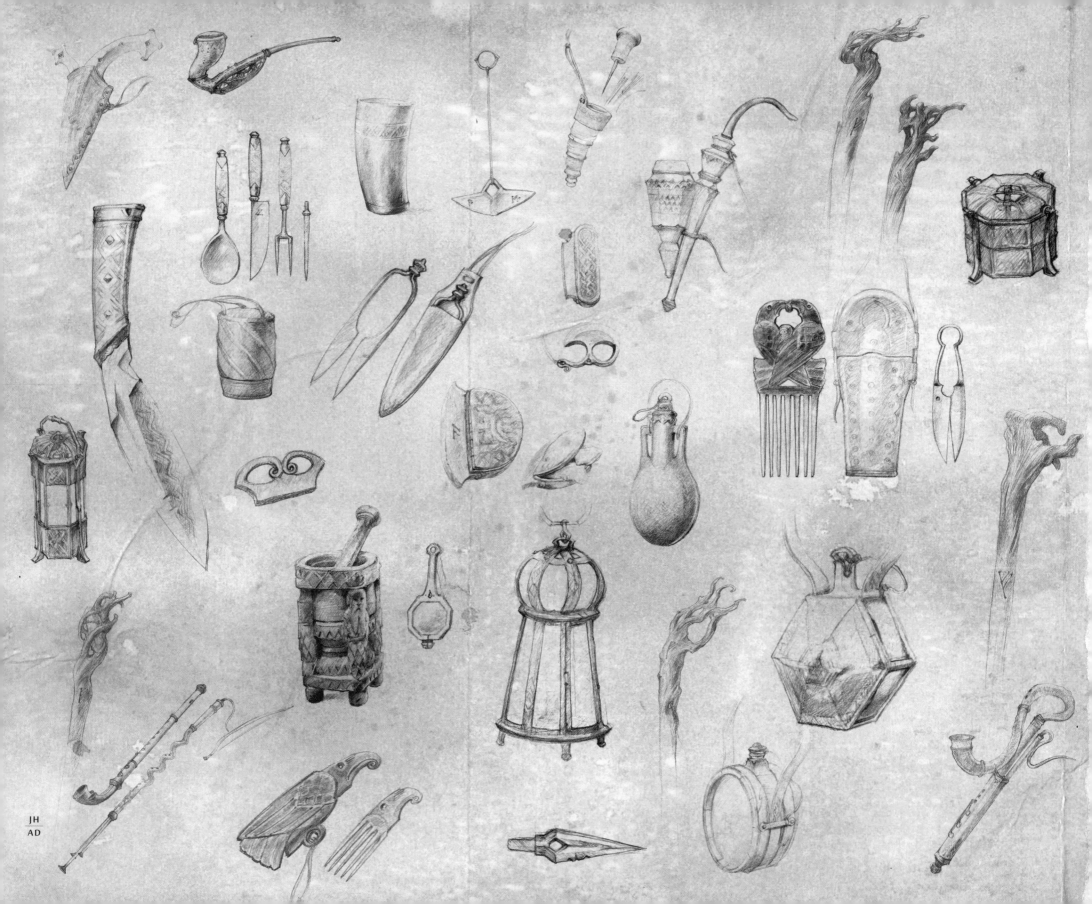

THE HOBBIT

AN UNEXPECTED JOURNEY

CHRONICLES ❖ ART & DESIGN

HarperCollins books may be purchased for educational, business, or sales promotional use. For information please write: Special Markets Department, HarperCollins*Publishers*, 10 East 53rd Street, New York, NY 10022.

First published in 2012 by:
Harper Design
An Imprint of HarperCollins*Publishers*
10 East 53rd Street
New York, NY 10022
Tel: (212) 207-7000
Fax: (212) 207 7654

Library of Congress Cataloging-in-Publication Data is available upon request.

ISBN: 978-0-06-220090-7

Printed and bound in China

First printing, 2012

Cover design by Monique Hamon
Back cover art by Gus Hunter
Spine art by Paul Tobin
Imprint page illustration by Alan Lee

Other publications from Weta include:

The Art of the Adventures of Tintin
The Art of District 9
Weta, The Collector's Guide
The Crafting of Narnia: The Art, Creatures, and Weapons from Weta Workshop
The World of Kong: A Natural History of Skull Island

Visit the Weta Workshop website for news, online shop and much more at www.wetaNZ.com

THE HOBBIT

AN UNEXPECTED JOURNEY

CHRONICLES ✦ ART & DESIGN

FOREWORD BY DAN HENNAH

INTRODUCTION BY RICHARD TAYLOR
WRITTEN BY DANIEL FALCONER

HARPER
DESIGN

An Imprint of HarperCollinsPublishers

WETA

www.wetaNZ.com

Contents

Acknowledgements

The Hobbit: An Unexpected Journey is a film of mind-blowing complexity and detail. The depth of artistic and technical consideration that has gone into creating it is impossible to comprehend, so it demanded a worthy art book companion. We have done our very best to meet that challenge and I am extremely proud of what we have achieved, but it came about because everyone involved shared that appreciation and went above and beyond to make it happen. In writing this book I relied to a very significant degree upon people pivotal to the production, people who were buried up to their beards in the business of making some of the most technically ambitious movies ever conceived!

It is therefore with the sincerest gratitude that I take the time here to acknowledge the contributions of those who gave so generously to help in the research and crafting of this book. It is no exaggeration to say we wouldn't have the book you hold in your hands if not for the support of these fine people.

First and foremost, I must thank Peter Jackson, Fran Walsh, Philippa Boyens and the film's producers for their indomitable creative vision, crafting the world of Middle-earth so lovingly and with such attention to detail. For me, both working on the movies and researching and crafting this book has been a truly sumptuous experience. There's just so much great stuff here. My thanks to them for the access and openness I have enjoyed while pulling the book together.

Sincerest thanks to the incredible Weta Publishing team, especially Kate Jorgensen and Monique Hamon, whose good humour and diligence have made working with them so easy and such a pleasure. Thanks also to Chris Smith, David Brawn, Terence Caven and the team at HarperCollins*Publishers* UK for their guidance, support and enthusiasm, as well as Jill Benscoter, Susannah Scott, Elaine Piechowski, Victoria Selover and Melanie Swartz

at Warner Bros, and Matt Dravitzki at Wingnut Films and Judy Alley at 3 Foot 7 Ltd for their help with approvals.

Specific thanks to Dan Hennah for his opening contribution and the invaluable advice and feedback he provided throughout the book's journey to completion.

I am very grateful to those across all the departments who have facilitated our access to artists and art resources, often at very short notice and while juggling their significant responsibilities on the film itself. These key individuals are named in full in the credits section at the back of this book.

Weta's Richard Taylor, Tania Rodger and Tim Launder have been stalwart enthusiasts for all our ongoing publishing initiatives and their unfaltering support is deeply appreciated.

And speaking of unfaltering support, thanks to my dear wife Catherine for tolerating the late nights and lost weekends I spent married to the book instead of being with my family.

Finally, this book is all about art and the artists who have created it. I am deeply appreciative for the time and insights that all who have their work in here have given us, but also to the many artists who aren't covered by this volume. On a project that has spanned so many years, been through such an evolution and for which many thousands of pieces of artwork have been produced, there are many more contributors than we could ever hope to adequately pay tribute to in one book. My thanks to those patient and diligent souls who, for whatever reason, may not find their work or commentary in these pages. Their contribution has been no less worthy and we hope they can take equal pride in the result, an amazing film and a pretty darn good art book.

Thanks everyone,
Daniel Falconer

FOREWORD

The Hobbit was always going to be a demanding film with regard to the Art Direction. JRR Tolkien's novel is so full of whimsical environments and fantastic creatures, not to mention the diverse races of Men, Elves, Dwarves and hobbits and their particular environs.

All told, in the script for the films there are over 120 set pieces as well as all the location environments. Not surprising when you realize that *The Hobbit* films are essentially road movies, which start in the Shire and go east for six months. As well as the changing seasons, from midsummer in Hobbiton to mid winter in Dale, the terrain and architecture also change. If you were to travel east from England to Tibet you might find some of the influences we used to illustrate the cultures of eastern Middle-earth.

The journey east influences our structures and cultures, form, texture and palette used to accentuate that journey.

To accomplish the journey we assembled a team of artists and craftspeople who immersed themselves in the cultures and crafts of Middle-earth. For three years these artists have been obsessing with the vagaries of the races, the architecture, the tools and weapons, terrain and vehicles of *The Hobbit*. It has very much been a full immersion into Tolkien's world for all of them. The contribution from all of our talented team requires an understanding of not only the cultures of hobbits and Dwarves but also the cultures that Bilbo and the Dwarves encounter on their journey.

In a fantasy world such as this there are no recipes, reference books, prop stores, costume stores or wig and mask stores that can do justice to the images conjured up by our director, Peter Jackson, and his collaborators. This means that every item had to be manufactured in our various workshops scattered around the Miramar peninsula.

Film is a collaborative medium and requires the complete attention of every person involved to find the images that will make the final cut. Each artist is encouraged to bring their individual vision to the project and work it in with others to make a cohesive part of the big picture. It is through this integration on every level that we are able to produce the series of exciting images that you see on the screen.

For a fantasy movie to succeed, it must transport the viewer into a totally believable world where Dwarves, Dragons, Wizards, Elves, Goblins, Orcs, Trolls and hobbits all exist in a seamless mix of complementary environments.

This book describes one essential step in the complex pursuit of making a great fantasy movie and introduces some of the artists involved in that pursuit.

Dan Hennah,
Production Designer

INTRODUCTION

If you have picked up this book, showcasing just some of the stunning work that so many have created for *The Hobbit: An Unexpected Journey*, the first film in Peter Jackson's adaptation of the enduringly popular masterpiece *The Hobbit*, by JRR Tolkien, then you most likely already have a great love of all things Tolkien and Middle-earth. You would therefore understand what a thrill it was for all of us at Weta Workshop, who similarly fell in love with this world, to once again be invited to be a part of Peter Jackson's film adaptations of JRR Tolkien's writing.

We produced a huge body of work for *The Lord of the Rings* over the seven years we spent on the film trilogy, but in imagining *The Hobbit* we would produce even more. Complementing the amazing production design and world creation of Dan Hennah and the Art Department, the costume designs of Ann Maskrey and Bob Buck, and the make-up work of Peter King and his crew, the Weta Workshop crew and I have revelled in this process and collaboration. Weta Workshop's design department alone would produce over 9000 paintings, conceptual drawings and design maquettes, many of which we share in this book and subsequent volumes in this series.

The Hobbit experience has again captured the magic and wonderment we found in our first foray into Tolkien's world. Written as it was by Tolkien for his children, *The Hobbit* has a different flavour to *The Lord of the Rings* and it has been interesting finding the visual voice of these films. We have enjoyed helping Peter realize the uniqueness of this story by designing the cast of characters that has brought his script to life.

On a personal note, JRR Tolkien's *The Hobbit* has a very special place in my heart – possibly even more so than *The Lord of the Rings* – as having read this book at a young age, this magical piece of literature has now remained with me for nearly four decades. Therefore being able to share in the experience of making these films is one that I treasure, and likewise sharing our collective work with you throughout this beautiful book that Daniel, Kate and Monique have put together, is something that all of us at Weta Workshop are very proud to do.

Richard Taylor,
Weta Workshop Design & Special Effects Supervisor

GH
WW

In a Hole in the Ground ...

... THERE LIVED A HOBBIT.

The story of *The Hobbit: An Unexpected Journey* begins, just as *The Fellowship of the Ring* did, in the gently rolling green-swathed hills of The Shire, dotted with cosy underground dwellings and cherubic, rosy-faced hobbits. Bag End is again the warm and inviting abode of Mister Bilbo Baggins and entering the stately burrow in The Hill is like returning home to a close friend or family.

Just as it did in preparation for the filming of the trilogy, work on the Hobbiton site began a year earlier in order to permit landscaping to settle and plantings to take and spread, conveying an appropriate and authentic lived-in feeling. The huge outdoor set had been dismantled and removed after filming on *The Lord of the Rings* was completed, leaving only yawning skeletal frames in the hillsides. Nonetheless, it had proven a very popular destination for tourists, so a plan was arranged that would see the rebuilding and expansion of the set for *The Hobbit* engineered as a permanent attraction with the empty hobbit holes rebuilt in lasting materials and screen-accurate. This would require craftspeople working in very different materials to those of traditional set building, in which a given environment need only last as long as the shoot at that location.

Not simply replicating the old sets, the crew would also be expanding and improving upon them wherever they could. Both the interior and exteriors of Bag End, for example, were expanded, and new holes added to Hobbiton. Changes were made to reflect the different time periods being represented during the shoot, with some scenes being set decades before others. And of course, this vision of Middle-earth had the added complication of being filmed at the higher frame rate of 48 frames per second and in 3D, demanding even greater attention to detail.

So began the rebuilding of Middle-earth, bigger and better than before, by a crew and cast comprised of familiar and new faces. New challenges and adventures were now in store both on screen and behind it.

BILBO

COSTUME

AM / CD

Soon after I joined the project I began cutting things out to make a start: coats, waistcoats and trousers. I created a show-and-tell selection of hobbit costumes with six or seven on stands for Peter Jackson, Fran Walsh and Philippa Boyens. Phil and Fran thought they were going in the right direction: then Peter quietly took a jacket from one stand and placed it over the waistcoat on another stand and then selected a pair of pants from a third. 'These are Bilbo's colours,' he said, and they have remained his colours ever since. Even after producing many other toiles of different variations, they eventually came back to these same colours and clothes I had started on my second day in New Zealand. We went a long way around but ended up back at the start. There and back again ..so to speak.

Bilbo's wardrobe, as compared to the other hobbits, is more that of a refined country gentleman, a bit more fastidious. Old Bilbo, as played by Sir Ian Holm, was in his established costume, designed by *The Lord of the Rings* Costume Designer Ngila Dickson.

Ann Maskrey, Costume Designer

AM / CD

MS / AD

AM / CD

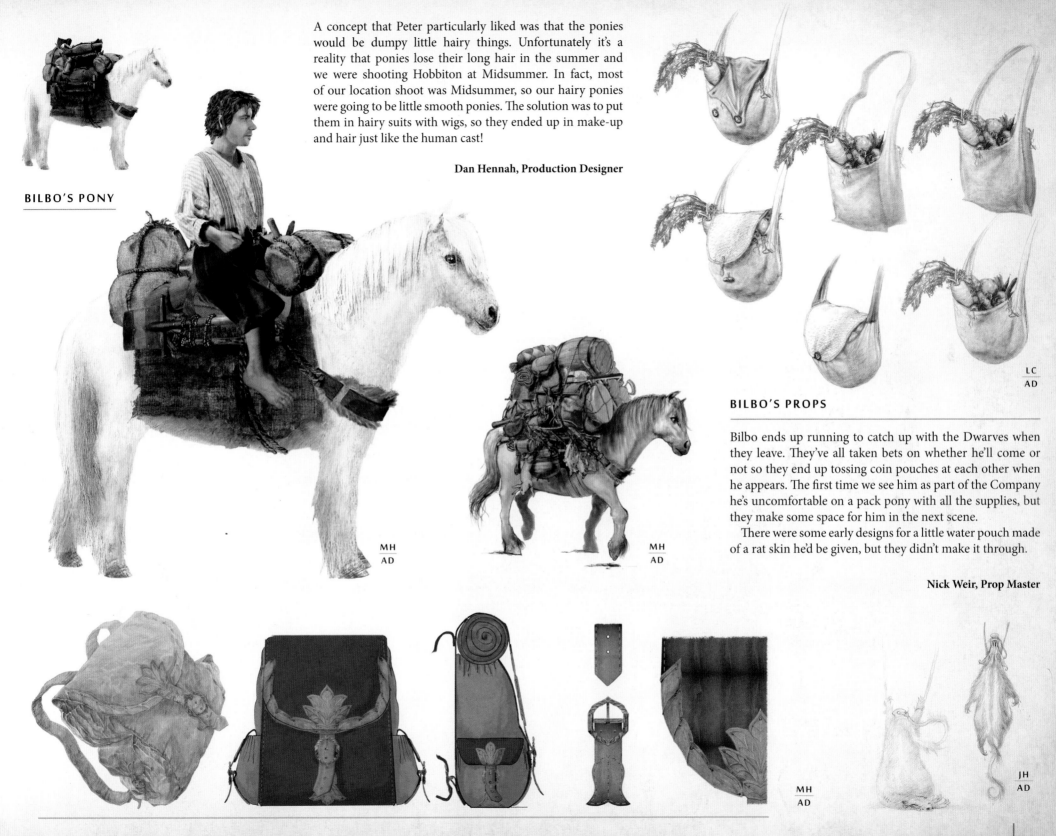

A concept that Peter particularly liked was that the ponies would be dumpy little hairy things. Unfortunately it's a reality that ponies lose their long hair in the summer and we were shooting Hobbiton at Midsummer. In fact, most of our location shoot was Midsummer, so our hairy ponies were going to be little smooth ponies. The solution was to put them in hairy suits with wigs, so they ended up in make-up and hair just like the human cast!

Dan Hennah, Production Designer

BILBO'S PONY

BILBO'S PROPS

Bilbo ends up running to catch up with the Dwarves when they leave. They've all taken bets on whether he'll come or not so they end up tossing coin pouches at each other when he appears. The first time we see him as part of the Company he's uncomfortable on a pack pony with all the supplies, but they make some space for him in the next scene.

There were some early designs for a little water pouch made of a rat skin he'd be given, but they didn't make it through.

Nick Weir, Prop Master

BAG END

BAG END ADDITIONS

The original Bag End built for *The Lord of the Rings* was designed by Production Designer Grant Major, but didn't extend far beyond the pantry, parlour and kitchen. There was the back corridor as well, but we didn't see much of it. For *The Hobbit*, we immediately had three new elements.

We had built the dining room for *The Lord of the Rings* but it wasn't seen, so we were able to redesign that room to work for 13 Dwarves, a hobbit and a wizard, plus build a pantry adjacent to it that would allow the all-important interaction between those two rooms as it plays out in the script.

Bilbo's bedroom was new, too, and there was his study, which plays a big part in linking the film series. It being 60 years earlier, we could lift the interior and redress it to add a bit more brightness.

Approaching Bag End as a whole, we introduced more vibrancy and colour. This is young Bilbo's home. It's not the house of an older gentleman who is looking after his nephew, so we embraced a rich look with a brighter palette across the board, including fabrics and textures, with velvet and lace. If there was a period influence to the design aesthetic, it would probably be Victiorian, as befit the references Tolkien hinted at with his mention of things like pocket watches.

The exterior design was very much the same, though we added a few more flowers and some other little details, but essentially it is the same place.

Dan Hennah, Production Designer

BAG END PARLOUR

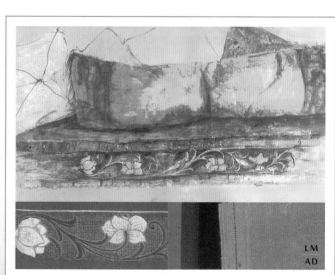

BAG END DINING ROOM

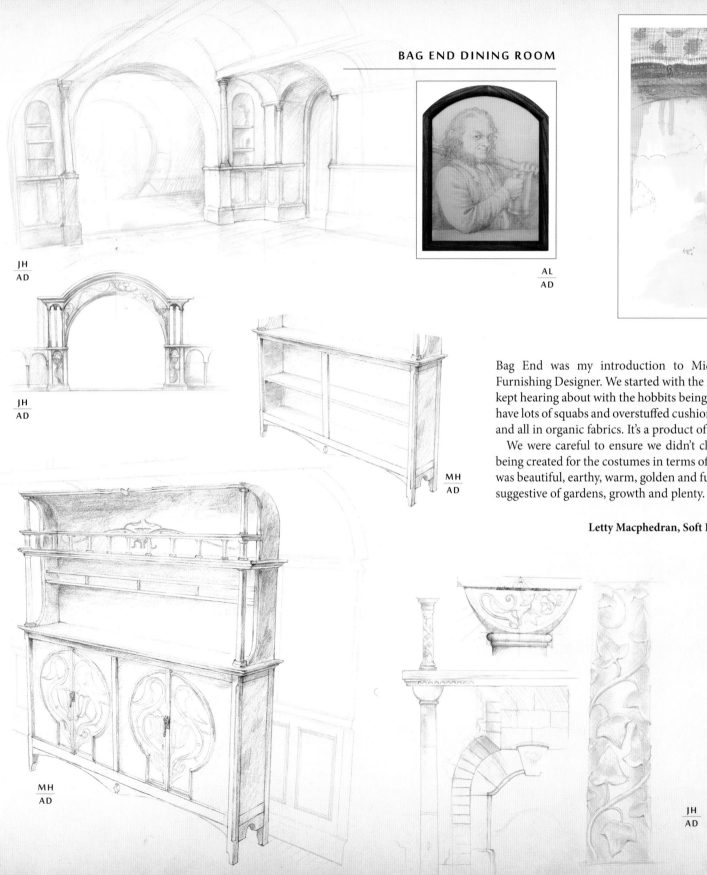

JH/AD

JH/AD

JH/AD

MH/AD

MH/AD

AL/AD

LM/AD

Bag End was my introduction to Middle-earth as Soft Furnishing Designer. We started with the idea of everything I kept hearing about with the hobbits being about comfort. We have lots of squabs and overstuffed cushions, lush furnishings and all in organic fabrics. It's a product of cottage industry.

We were careful to ensure we didn't clash with what was being created for the costumes in terms of colour. The palette was beautiful, earthy, warm, golden and full of natural greens suggestive of gardens, growth and plenty.

Letty Macphedran, Soft Furnishing Designer

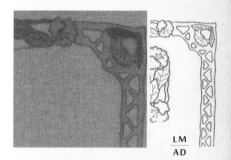

LM/AD

For a scene with Frodo and an older Bilbo, the filmmakers wanted audiences to see something in Bag End and be able to identify it as something Bilbo had brought back from his travels. I drew a concept for a tooth, claw or spur that looked dragonish. At this point in the story it is left a little ambiguous exactly what it is, but the implication is that it is from Smaug.

Alan Lee, Concept Art Director

AL/AD

MH
AD

JH
AD

BAG END DINING ROOM

We designed and made a lot of new furniture. You can't go out and buy hobbit furniture and certainly not at two scales, which so much of our stuff had to be built at, so it's our normal process to design, approve and build everything.

Where we were making new stuff we had to stay in the same environment, so it had to feel like what we'd seen before, but one thing we did that was a little different this time was try some slightly more exotic timbers. Now there is chestnut, elm, oak and ash in Bag End. We knew what Bag End looked like and so we knew what we were looking for and could go looking for these kinds of variations, knowing where it was going to go.

Nick Weir, Prop Master

JH
AD

BILBO'S BEDROOM

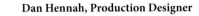

We never saw Bilbo's bedroom in *The Lord of the Rings*. For *The Hobbit*, we added it a little further round the hill from the front door, a cosy and comfortable little room with inviting, warm colours.

Dan Hennah, Production Designer

MH / AD

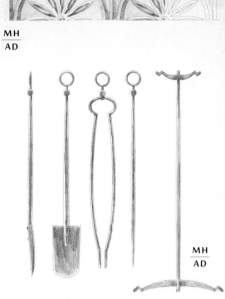

MH / AD

MH / AD

AM / CD

LM / AD

MH / AD

One of the wonderful things about making *The Hobbit* was the opportunity to not only re-make everything faithfully, but also to put in sixty years of freshness. We have stepped back in time and everything is a bit newer, more light-hearted and a bit more colourful. With Bilbo's bedroom being a new set, we could start from scratch, which was quite liberating, so there's lots of colour and new textures in there. We tied the furniture and architecture together with some gorgeous drapes and window treatments, which were just made for a cosy bedroom.

Ra Vincent, Set Decorator

LM / AD

MH / AD

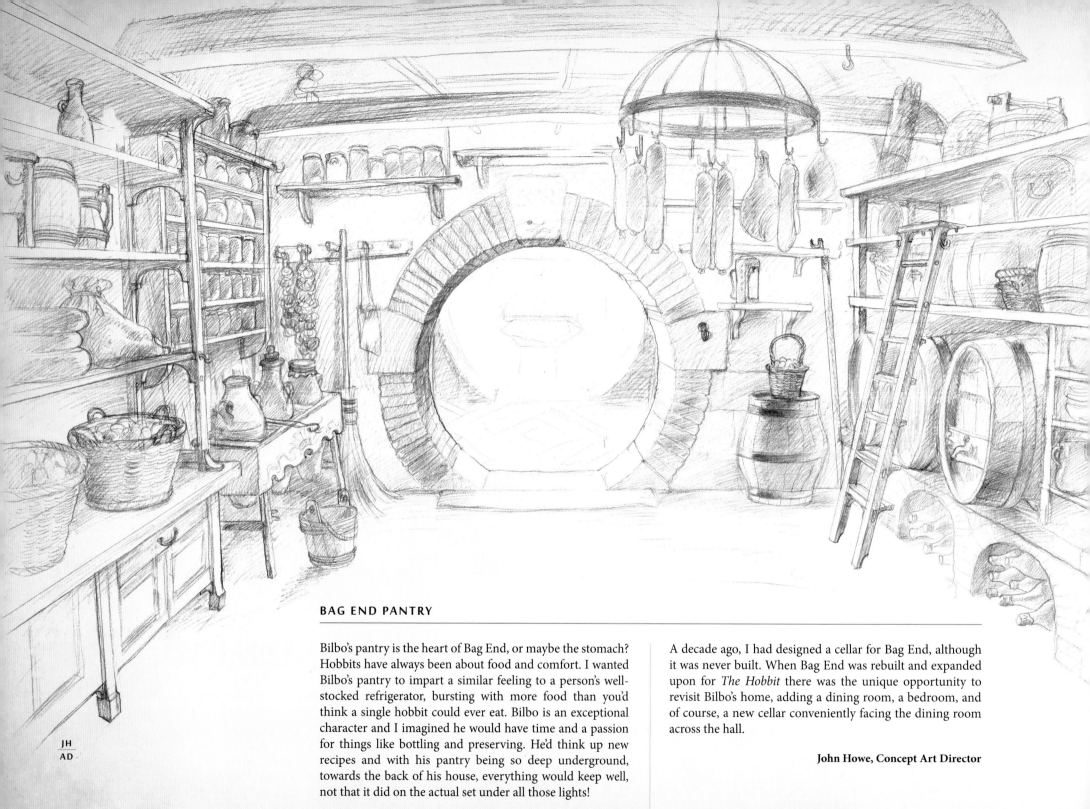

BAG END PANTRY

Bilbo's pantry is the heart of Bag End, or maybe the stomach? Hobbits have always been about food and comfort. I wanted Bilbo's pantry to impart a similar feeling to a person's well-stocked refrigerator, bursting with more food than you'd think a single hobbit could ever eat. Bilbo is an exceptional character and I imagined he would have time and a passion for things like bottling and preserving. He'd think up new recipes and with his pantry being so deep underground, towards the back of his house, everything would keep well, not that it did on the actual set under all those lights!

Ra Vincent, Set Decorator

A decade ago, I had designed a cellar for Bag End, although it was never built. When Bag End was rebuilt and expanded upon for *The Hobbit* there was the unique opportunity to revisit Bilbo's home, adding a dining room, a bedroom, and of course, a new cellar conveniently facing the dining room across the hall.

John Howe, Concept Art Director

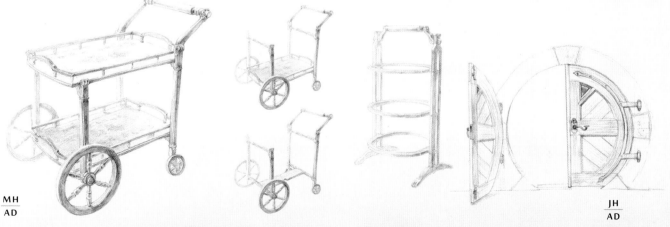

BILBO'S DRESSING GOWN

Made of many different fabrics, Bilbo's dressing gown is a favourite with everyone, including actor Martin Freeman. There are silks, wools, brocades, chenille and velvet. The apparently random patchwork had to be very carefully mapped out so as not to end up with matching blocks of colour ending up together that could be distracting to the eye.

Ann Maskrey, Costume Designer

HOBBITS

Before travelling to Matamata for the Hobbiton location shoot we had one day shooting in Wellington with Little Bilbo, his mother Belladonna, Old Hob, Old Gammidge and Bilbo's grandfather, the Old Took. They have a little chat over a drink when Gandalf arrives – quite a nice scene actually. It was very picturesque with hobbits outside under a tent enjoying a half-pint, young girls dancing, a bit of colourful magic that set the scene for later events.

Ann Maskrey, Costume Designer

While we tried to maintain continuity with what went before we also took the opportunity to refresh our hobbits a bit. They're not just little funny short people with furry feet. We really tried to create characters. Their ears are a little pointier and more defined, less cauliflower ear-like.

Our girl hobbits are a little prettier this time around. Ann Maskrey had created frocks that were sort of Eighteenth Century inspired, so we did the same with their hair. Instead of just curly hair, we gave them all styles.

Peter King, Make-up and Hair Designer

AM
CD

AM
CD

AM
CD

AM/BB
CD

AM
CD

COSTUMES

I wanted to get more colour into the hobbits than we had seen before. Fran Walsh was keen to see some jewel colours in their costumes. We also discovered as we went along that the red camera has a tendency to sludge things down, so we have pushed more colour back in there to compensate. Belladonna Took is a new character, so we had free reign with her.

Ann Maskrey, Costume Designer

Lobelia Sackville-Baggins' costume tells you so much about her with just a glance. She aspires to be the best dressed lady in Hobbiton, but she gets it slightly wrong and comes off overdone. Her colours are bright and show-offy. She's decked out like an old traveller's caravan with a mad hat, brolly and bag. Otho Sackville-Baggins is basically told what to wear by his wife.

Ann Maskrey, Costume Designer

HOBBIT PROSTHETICS

We revisited the hobbits' ears, doing Photoshop exercises to explore options that Peter could chose from. We very slightly exaggerated everything this time round, so the ears were a little bit larger and the feet of our hobbits were a little longer than before, as well.

Greg Tozer, Weta Workshop Designer

HOBBITON

HOBBIT HOLES

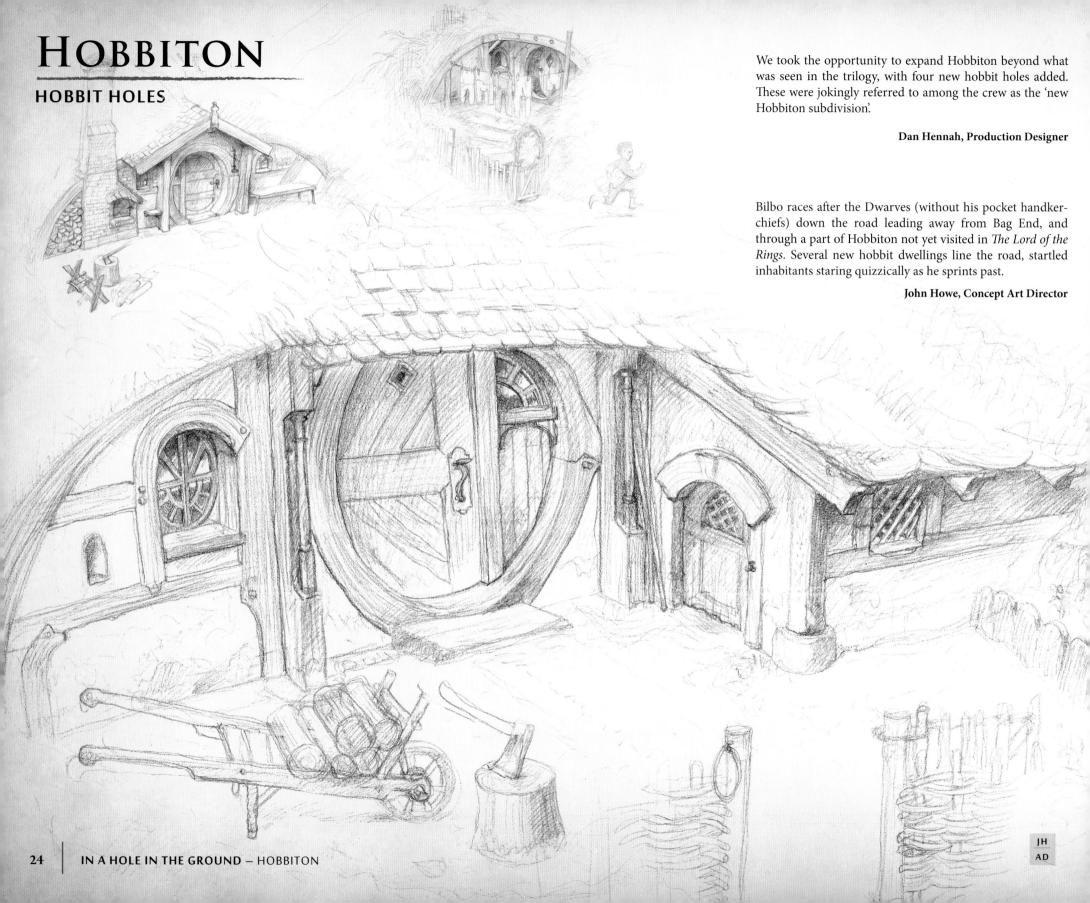

We took the opportunity to expand Hobbiton beyond what was seen in the trilogy, with four new hobbit holes added. These were jokingly referred to among the crew as the 'new Hobbiton subdivision'.

Dan Hennah, Production Designer

Bilbo races after the Dwarves (without his pocket handkerchiefs) down the road leading away from Bag End, and through a part of Hobbiton not yet visited in *The Lord of the Rings*. Several new hobbit dwellings line the road, startled inhabitants staring quizzically as he sprints past.

John Howe, Concept Art Director

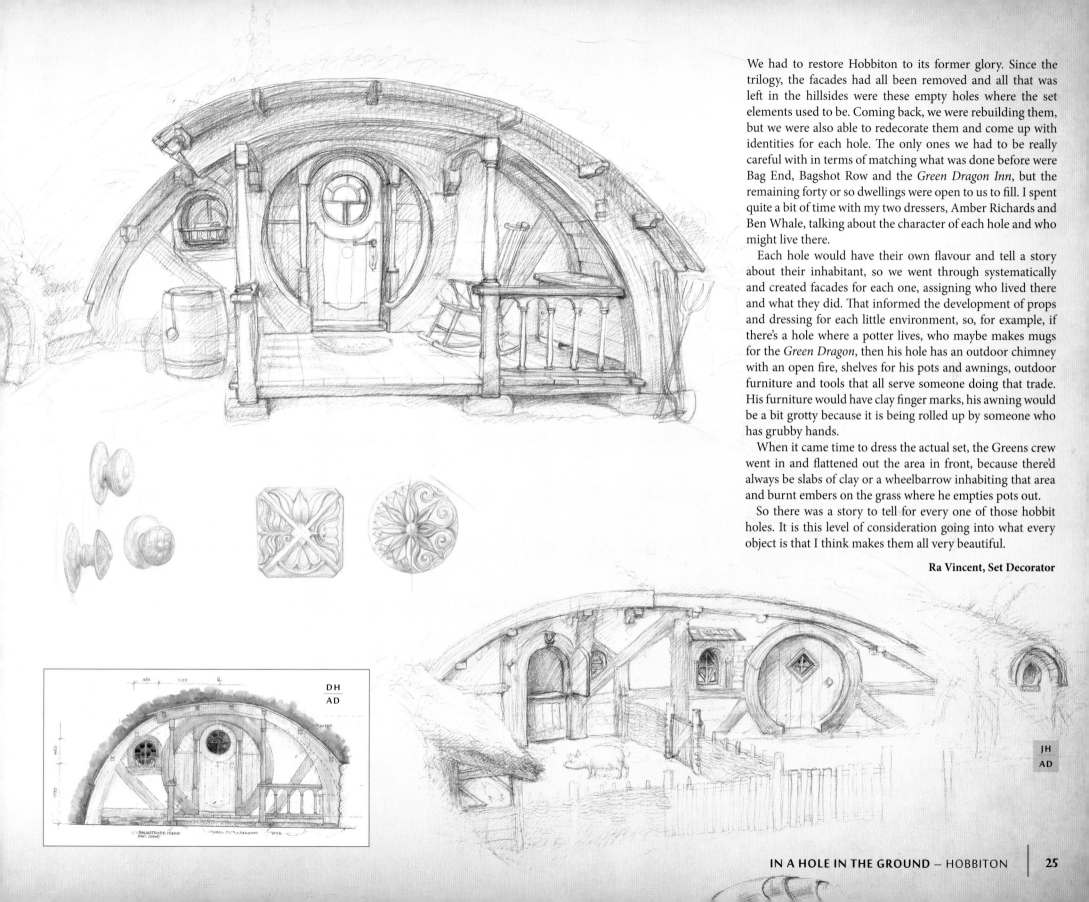

We had to restore Hobbiton to its former glory. Since the trilogy, the facades had all been removed and all that was left in the hillsides were these empty holes where the set elements used to be. Coming back, we were rebuilding them, but we were also able to redecorate them and come up with identities for each hole. The only ones we had to be really careful with in terms of matching what was done before were Bag End, Bagshot Row and the *Green Dragon Inn*, but the remaining forty or so dwellings were open to us to fill. I spent quite a bit of time with my two dressers, Amber Richards and Ben Whale, talking about the character of each hole and who might live there.

Each hole would have their own flavour and tell a story about their inhabitant, so we went through systematically and created facades for each one, assigning who lived there and what they did. That informed the development of props and dressing for each little environment, so, for example, if there's a hole where a potter lives, who maybe makes mugs for the *Green Dragon*, then his hole has an outdoor chimney with an open fire, shelves for his pots and awnings, outdoor furniture and tools that all serve someone doing that trade. His furniture would have clay finger marks, his awning would be a bit grotty because it is being rolled up by someone who has grubby hands.

When it came time to dress the actual set, the Greens crew went in and flattened out the area in front, because there'd always be slabs of clay or a wheelbarrow inhabiting that area and burnt embers on the grass where he empties pots out.

So there was a story to tell for every one of those hobbit holes. It is this level of consideration going into what every object is that I think makes them all very beautiful.

Ra Vincent, Set Decorator

THE GREEN DRAGON INN AND MARKET

RV
AD

Hobbiton's *Green Dragon Inn* was established in *The Lord of the Rings*. This time round, going back again and rebuilding it, we decided to give it more of a spring or summer look, so rather than having a big gravel yard out the front we planted a lot more grass. This is sixty years earlier than last time we saw it so it's a credible difference.

We also put in paving tiles. One of the things we decided to do early on with Hobbiton was not to use shingle. It's easy and not a perverse thing to use, but with a year to cultivate and prepare the site before filming we felt we could do better, so we paved the paths and put grass in between the pavers.

Dan Hennah, Production Designer

JH
AD

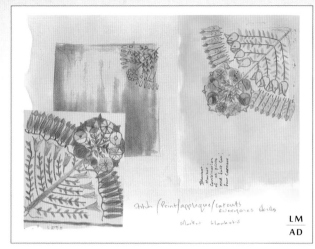

The next time someone remarks how little we know of centuries past, I'll have a story to tell. We ended up redrawing most of the sculpture details for the *Green Dragon Inn*, simply because there were no documents showing the original set with any clarity. Many of the details were variations on a theme, done directly on site by the sculptors, and no one thought to take photos – and this on one of the most popular films ever made.

Coming back a decade along, new drawings for the new carvings around the doorways, posts and window frames, wracking our brains trying to recall what was originally done. We drew on pastoral themes: barley and grapes, all sheaves and twining vines, very green and growing, or ripe for the harvest.

John Howe, Concept Art Director

For the market day scene we filled the court outside the *Green Dragon* with extras and lots and lots of props. There were entertainers and stalls, and picnicking hobbits. It was more than just a market, it was a party, and hobbits love those. We were able to resurrect numerous props from *The Lord of the Rings*, but there was also a huge amount of new stuff that Ra Vincent and John Howe came up with, designed and had our teams execute.

We played up big elements like large animals, giant mugs, a turkey to stand in for a roast chicken, and big pumpkins, all in an effort to make the hobbits look small. This was all about convincing the viewers that hobbits are small. If this is established very strongly right at the beginning then it tends not to be questioned later in the film.

Dan Hennah, Production Designer

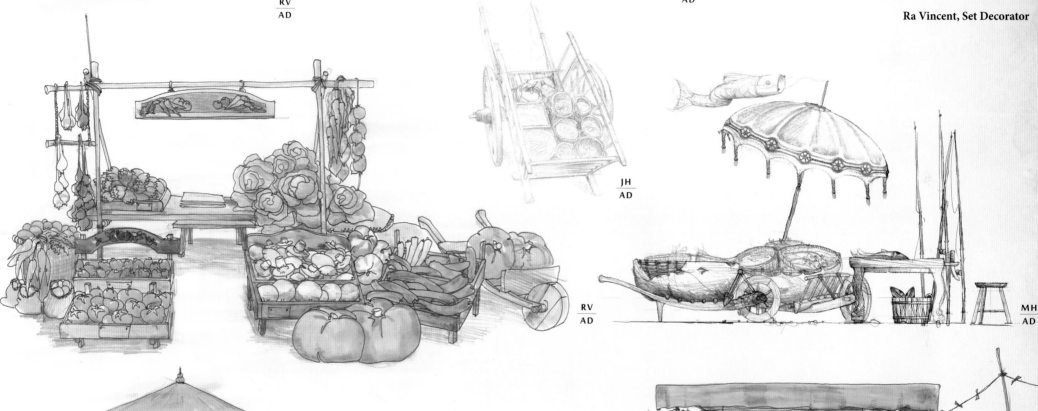

MARKET PROPS

In preparation for the delightful Hobbiton summer market scene I took some leads from Alan Lee and John Howe's beautiful conceptual art. They had drawn lots of gorgeous character stalls with hobbits making and selling their wares or trades. I worked up colour treatments from their drawings, but also found opportunities to explore the spaces in between with big features that I would design.

Ra Vincent, Set Decorator

RV / AD

MH / AD

JH / AD

RV / AD

MH / AD

RV / AD

RV / AD

THE OLD TOOK'S PARTY

AL
AD

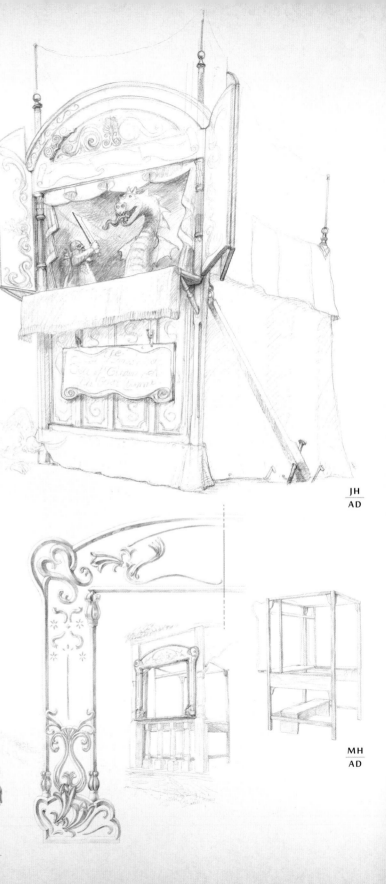

JH
AD

JH
AD

Gandalf and Bilbo first meet when Bilbo is just a little lad at the Old Took's party. It's a midsummer celebration in the orchard near the lake, put on by the Old Took for the children with a Punch and Judy show, fireworks and beer for the parents.

Gandalf plays a little trick and pulls a dragon out of his sleeve. All the other children run away, but Bilbo stays and is intrigued by the dragon, giving Gandalf the impression of a rather courageous little hobbit. And of course it was fun for me, as I got to play the Old Took!

Dan Hennah, Production Designer

MH
AD

MH
AD

The party was really fun and turned out to be so pretty with the tents. We had a little Punch and Judy puppet show for the hobbit children and created some little puppets for it. Though we didn't use the Troll in the end, he may yet find his way into some other part of Middle-earth.

Ra Vincent, Set Decorator

LC
AD

IN A HOLE IN THE GROUND – THE OLD TOOK'S PARTY | 31

AN UNEXPECTED PARTY

INTRODUCING THE COMPANY OF THORIN

Into Bilbo Baggins' world would tumble a company of Dwarves whom he would find himself joining on a quest across Middle-earth. The Dwarves' boisterous arrival in his tidy little home signals the obliteration of Bilbo's peaceful existence and the beginning of the adventure proper. As they arrive audiences meet the unusually large cast of characters who would propel Bilbo along his journey and through many misfortunes before it was done.

The Dwarves represented a huge challenge to every department involved in helping define their portrayal for the screen. Audiences had an expectation of what a Dwarf might look like after spending three films getting to know Gimli. Gimli, however, was but one Dwarf in a Fellowship of many races, so he could corner all that was dwarfy and claim it as his own in *The Lord of the Rings*. For *The Hobbit*, there would be thirteen Dwarves in the main cast and many more besides in supporting roles. They could not all be clones of Gimli. Each needed to honour the archetype that he embodied, but bring their own unique characterization and be immediately recognizable to even casual movie goers, no easy task considering that most of the thirteen were only loosely defined in the original book.

Each Dwarf would demand his own distinctive appearance, reflecting his characterisation in the scripts, but there was also the issue of Dwarf proportions. Dwarves are by definition short and burly, so a large part of the design challenge faced by the many contributing departments would be to find ways to transform the widely varied regular height cast of humans into a different species.

Dwarven clothing, weapons and equipment cannot be purchased at any store. So everything they wore, carried or fought with had to be conceived and constructed in such a way that not only worked in an individual fashion, but also painted a broader picture of a single, multi-faceted culture as vibrant and believable as any real world society, yet be immediately and distinctly recognizable as Dwarven.

It was an undertaking that would see all the departments working very closely together under the astute stewardship of Peter Jackson and his writing partners Fran Walsh and Philippa Boyens as they honed and refined the characters that would populate and propel their films.

PHOTOGRAPH (LEFT) BY JAMES FISHER

DWARVES

The Dwarves of *The Hobbit* had to be unique and iconic. Peter didn't want short humans – he wanted to see Dwarves, and that meant they had to have their own distinct bone structure and larger heads in relation to their body size, because that is what you expect in someone under five feet tall. However, we had a cast of actors of whom many were more like six feet tall, meaning their proportions would be very different and much more of a challenge to cheat to look like stocky Dwarves.

So began our quest!

Richard Taylor,
Weta Workshop Design & Special Effects Supervisor

While designs for specific Dwarves would come later, in the beginning we experimented with how much or little could be done with prosthetics to give a person the impression of a Dwarf. We made sketches but also used Photoshop on photographs of crewmembers to try out different styles of noses and beards to see how extreme we could make them.

Alan Lee, Concept Art Director

We began our Dwarf process in earnest with Photoshop paint-overs on a number of crew members of diverse types. How far could we push our augmentations and could we turn someone very unlike a Dwarf into a convincing character? Could we produce handsome Dwarves or would they always be big-nosed and comedic looking?

Richard Taylor,
Weta Workshop Design & Special Effects Supervisor

Long noses, droopy beards and moustaches, widely spaced ears and broadened craniums all helped make our Dwarves' heads appear larger and help suggest their smaller stature. A Dwarf should probably have a five-to-one body to head ratio, whereas someone six-foot-three is more likely to have an eight to one ratio.

Once we started getting casting confirmations we began Photoshop exercises on the actual actors' images, a process that Peter was intimately involved with all the way through. It was a delight seeing these characters emerging as we sought to not only turn them into Dwarves, but also to establish unique looks for each of them: we had great fun with elaborate hair and beard styles, ornamentation and prosthetics.

This process led us to Plasticine sculpts on the actors' head casts, once we had them, and these were hugely constructive in locking down the look of each character.

Richard Taylor,
Weta Workshop Design & Special Effects Supervisor

Alan Lee and I Photoshopped ourselves as Dwarves, kicking off a whole raft of Dwarven persona. I must admit that I stuck my frowning Dwarven face in every bit of concept art that could plausibly accept a Dwarf … alas, in vain, as I never got an audition. Actually, that's not true, I can't act to save my life; my view of Middle-earth is with sketchbook on my knees and pencils firmly in hand.

John Howe, Concept Art Director

When scaling props for Dwarf and hobbit-scaled doubles we had a ratio which was definitive. If Richard Armitage's Thorin required a prop of a certain length next to his arm, his small-scale double would require a duplicate prop that was the same proportion in relation to his shorter arm length. There was some fudging at times because of the shift in proportions that sometimes occurs when using doubles, but mostly we made any prop that would be required at Dwarf or human scales at two sizes, one being about 1.2 times the other.

Nick Weir, Prop Master

When we started on the Dwarves, Nick Keller initially created a series of paintings of each character in Thorin's Company. It was helpful to be able to react to them as a group and see where we needed to go. Peter rightly asserted that we had to find very distinctive silhouettes for every Dwarf. While they all had to be Dwarves, they also had to be individuals with their own iconic shapes and colours so they could be easily told apart. We pursued this intensely and that is how we ended up with such diversity among our thirteen.

We also had to find ways to modify their body shapes to give each of them Dwarven physiques. In addition to making their heads appear larger, we tried extensively to modify their body forms through the use of fat suits, lowered waistlines, widening shoulders, increasing their girth and giving them larger hands.

Peter's challenge to us was to accomplish our face and head augmentation without adding prosthetics to their cheeks or lower faces, keeping them only on the brows, scalp and noses, which would speed up make-up application time. On Gimli we added cheeks to help fill out and square up his face, but not doing this for the new Dwarves meant a very thoughtful approach to their designs was required. It was challenging, but great fun and, with so many characters to go around, almost everyone in our design department was able to get involved and latch onto a favourite Dwarf.

Richard Taylor,
Weta Workshop Design & Special Effects Supervisor

Line-ups of the Company were essential when designing the Dwarves because each had to be distinctive. Peter had pursued general silhouette ideas with Weta Workshop, but these needed translating and the components explaining and defining. We also had to consider the many changes and layers, because, just as the characters did, so would our costumes undergo transformations along their journey, becoming more distressed with various layers being visible at different points in the story. They all needed different shirts underneath their travelling gear and cloaks, for example (below).

Tolkien assigned colours to the Dwarves' hoods and we were faithful to these with the insides of our hoods, but otherwise he wasn't too specific about their costumes, affording us plenty of scope to develop each character ourselves. This meant they were open to interpretation, but it also meant that everyone had an opinion, which sometimes made it difficult to narrow down! We worked up the Dwarves' boots and buckles in detail. Each of them reflects their owner's individuality as much as any other part of their costume. Patterning on fabrics was loosely based on Gimli's angular patterns, but we developed

many prints and patterns. Because we might not be able to buy a given variety of fabric in the right quantity, we'd instead sometimes buy a plain suede and put a puff print on it, for example, and assign it to Bofur, or a different one to Gloin. We burnt prints into some fabrics while other times we used a puff or a discharge print, varying it as much as possible so that they would look like a family, but with their own unique characteristics in keeping with the personalities that Peter, Fran and Philippa had devised.

Ann Maskrey, Costume Designer

THORIN

MAKE-UP AND HAIR

JFA
WW

AJB
WW

AJB
WW

DF
WW

GT
WW

PT
WW

PT
WW

PT
WW

GT
WW

PT
WW

PT
WW

PT
WW

It became clear after a comprehensive round of design and prosthetic prototyping that Peter, Fran and Philippa saw Thorin as being very handsome and noble, but in an unpretentious way. Our prosthetic work evolved to become very subtle, in some places only half a millimetre thick. This served to enhance and refine actor Richard Armitage's own features towards that refined nobility rather than impose a new look upon him, and included subtly straightening his nose and refining his brow.

Richard Taylor,
Weta Workshop Design & Special Effects Supervisor

Initially I think I went too elaborate with all the silver and plaiting in my first Thorin concepts, maybe too much like he was at a coronation. He needed a wilder look, less adorned and a bit younger, but I still pushed for some isolated greying.

Paul Tobin, Weta Workshop Designer

The design process begins with pictures. In Thorin's case there must have been hundreds done. Many were quite complicated, with decorative plaiting and jewellery, but as the process went on they became simplified. Peter, Fran and Philippa weren't imagining Thorin as a character who would ornament himself. We didn't know these characters when we started, but going through these processes their characters would emerge in reaction to what was proposed.

Even as close to the final look as the last concept was *(far right)*, he evolved once we were working with real hair and prosthetics on the actor.

Peter King, Make-up and Hair Designer

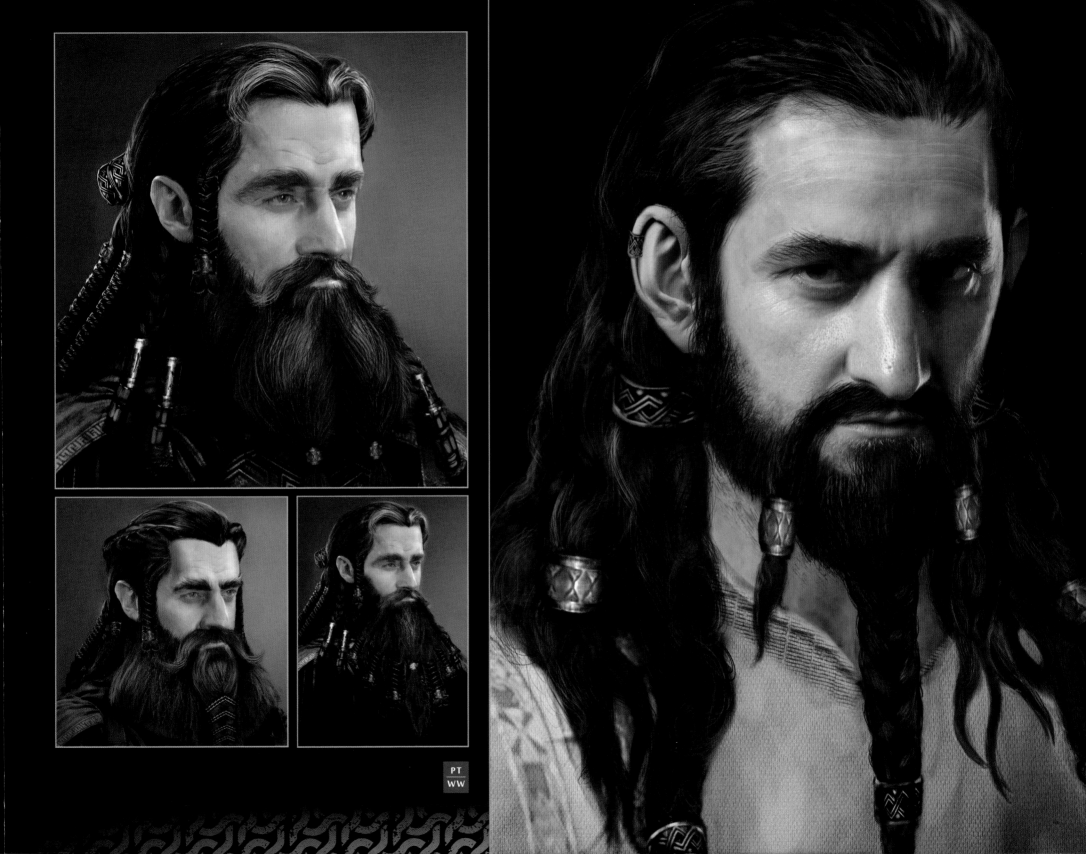

THORIN'S COSTUME

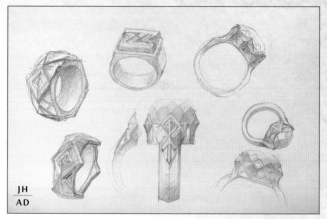

Thorin's ring is a ring of kingship, a seal and a symbol of his status, a bittersweet reminder that he is no longer King Under the Mountain, but a refugee wandering Middle-earth.

John Howe, Concept Art Director

There were going to be three travel rings worn by Thorin, Balin and Dwalin: something they had made while on the road that bound them together on this quest. Dwalin's didn't really work with his knuckle-dusters so we only ended up making Thorin's and the back story was dropped.

Nick Weir, Prop Master

Thorin's travelling costume had to make him look imposing, regal and yet dark. The midnight blue colour allocated to the character particularly suited Richard Armitage. I found one of his fabrics quite early on and it already had a very Dwarven figured imprint on the velvet. It only came in a very pale grey and before ordering it in bulk I had to see if we could dye it to his dark blue colour without the pattern disappearing, which thankfully it didn't. I tried to give each Dwarf his own particular form of decoration and Thorin is the only one to have this type of velvet.

Ann Maskrey, Costume Designer

We were coming up with broad shapes and cuts that might serve as inspiration for the costume designs, trying to very quickly find distinctive outlines for each character. I thought that some fur collars and edging might help create wide shoulders and help convey a royal stature.

Paul Tobin, Weta Workshop Designer

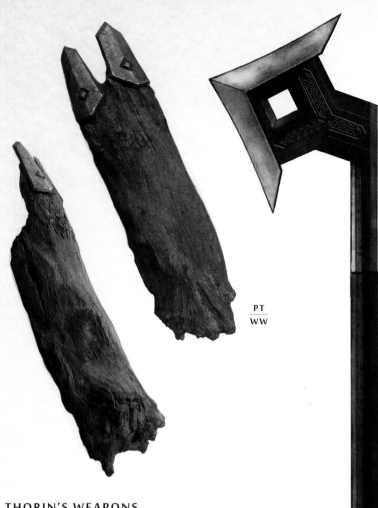

The faceting on Thorin's bow was another of those cues that had been established in *The Lord of the Rings* and worked so well to define something as being Dwarven. It was a kind of design shorthand that immediately said Dwarf.

Paul Tobin, Weta Workshop Designer

THORIN'S WEAPONS

Thorin receives the name Oakenshield when he is younger when, finding himself without a shield in the middle of dreadful battle, he breaks a branch off a tree and fights with it on his arm. I thought it would be nice to bring something from the past into what was happening now: he might have kept and nurtured this chunk of oak that had saved his life and perhaps honed it into something else. I made a sketch of it, like a branch that had been hollowed to become something like a vambrace with prongs, which I showed to Peter and he liked the idea of it.

Richard Taylor picked it up and we went through a development of the idea. It briefly had a fist-like end with nails in it, but it started to look Orcish so we pulled back from that to keep a Dwarvish feel.

Richard Armitage, Actor, Thorin

I originally designed Thorin's axe as a thrower for one of the other Dwarves who was going to have a pair of these, but Peter saw it and said, 'No, let's make one and let's make it big.' I think you can see its original purpose in its shape, but with a longer handle it looks great as Thorin's main axe.

Thorin's sword, 'Deathless', was what happens when I get to go crazy and design a sword that is right on the edge of going into total over-the-top fantasy, but hopefully just inside that edge. It's not a human weapon at all. I was doing my best to make it non-human. I drew a little selection of options and Peter picked the best one; at least, I think so.

Frank Victoria, Weta Workshop Designer

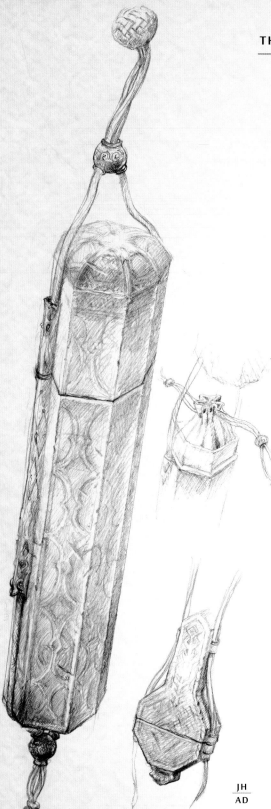

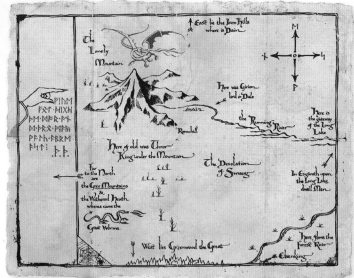

DR
AD

To maintain close continuity between films, this map had to closely resemble the version I created for *The Fellowship of the Ring*. The script – and aesthetic sensibilities – called for some minor changes in wording and geography, resulting in Thorin's map as seen in *The Hobbit*.

Daniel Reeve, Graphic Artist

JH
AD

THORIN'S KEY

I think I drew literally hundreds of ideas for Dwarven props, intent on kitting them out with everything they needed to be convincing as a troupe of resourceful individuals who have spent more than a century on the road. Some props, though, like Thorin's key, while having no quotidian and practical purpose, had to sum up what differentiates a household object with which we are all familiar from a special object that can open the back door to a mountain.

John Howe, Concept Art Director

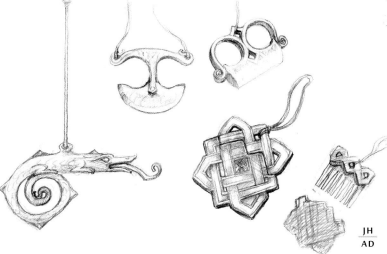

JH
AD

JH
AD

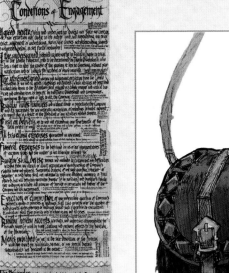

MH / AD

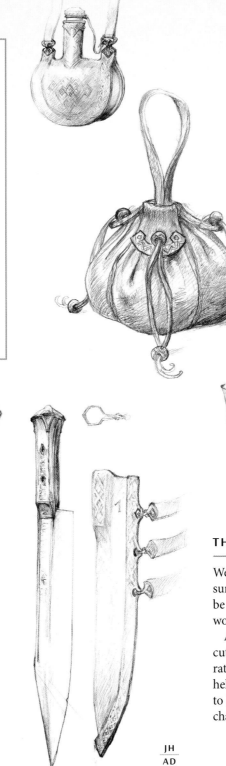

JH / AD

DR / AD

JH / AD

THORIN'S ACCOUTREMENTS

We worked a little bit with the Costume department, making sure that we all understood what the colours were going to be for each character as we were creating all their props so it would all work together.

All the Dwarves had their own unique cups, bowls and cutlery. Some were designed to be more like found items rather than from a Dwarf hardware store, occasionally barely held together with string. It's the kind of thing that is done to help give everything some age and history and make the characters unique and real.

Nick Weir, Prop Master

MAKE-UP, HAIR AND COSTUME

Balin's final beard design was originally conceived for Oin but Peter Jackson felt they were more suitable when switched.

I tried cheating up the size of the Dwarves' heads to make them seem more squat and traditionally Dwarven in proportions. Longer noses and droopy moustaches that hid the lips gave the illusion of lower mouths, which is what I was attempting with Oin, and then Balin, once the design shifted to him. I imagined a long moustache might also reinforce the character's dignity and sophistication.

Daniel Falconer, Weta Workshop Designer

While he ended up looking a lot like the concept imagery, once again we stripped elements out as we went along. A lot of important information comes from Balin in the films, so that was one of the reasons in the end why he didn't have a moustache. He didn't really need it. It was important to be able to see the actor giving his lines and expressing, and it was another point of difference from the rest.

Peter King, Make-up and Hair Designer

In the beginning we were looking for signature shapes that would distinguish each Dwarf. Balin's beard had a kind of ski-ramp flick, so taking that as his icon, I thought we might echo it in his coat, weapons and boots.

Daniel Falconer, Weta Workshop Designer

Balin needed to appear as the elder statesman of the group and his red and black woven leather belt is a particular favourite of mine. I was very fortunate to have such skilled leather workers on site and we made full use of their skills with the Dwarves in particular. Balin and Thorin also bore embroidery and more intricate decoration than their fellows, another way in which we subtly reinforced their elevated status among the Company.

Ann Maskrey, Costume Designer

BALIN'S WEAPONS AND PROPS

Sometimes the level of finish on a given prop related to the character's history or conveyed a sense of their prestige. Balin has a lectern to write upon while he rides *(right)*. It was oak, so we tried to do justice to the quality of the wood. It's a very nice prop, which fits for him, given the regal character that Balin is.

Nick Weir, Prop Master

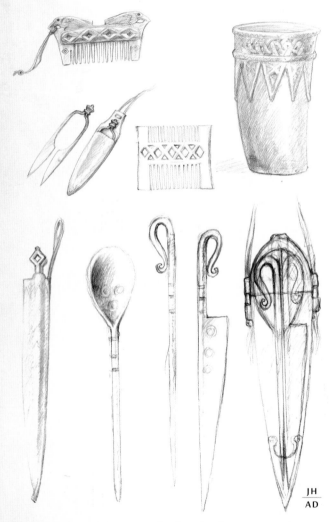

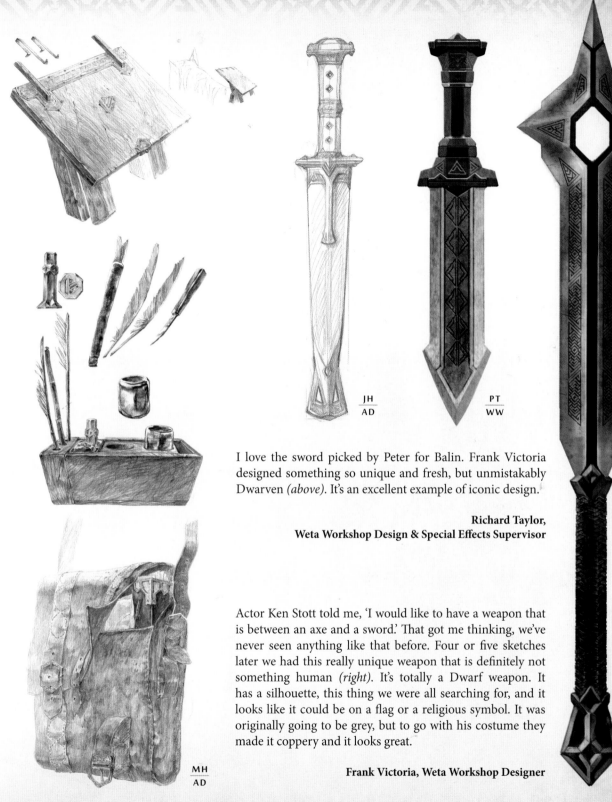

When we were coming up with ideas for the costume shapes I had a hit with my Balin concept *(opposite, bottom, second from left)*. They liked this one because it looked comfortable and elegant and it isn't too far off what was made in the end.

Frank Victoria, Weta Workshop Designer

I love the sword picked by Peter for Balin. Frank Victoria designed something so unique and fresh, but unmistakably Dwarven *(above)*. It's an excellent example of iconic design.

**Richard Taylor,
Weta Workshop Design & Special Effects Supervisor**

Actor Ken Stott told me, 'I would like to have a weapon that is between an axe and a sword.' That got me thinking, we've never seen anything like that before. Four or five sketches later we had this really unique weapon that is definitely not something human *(right)*. It's totally a Dwarf weapon. It has a silhouette, this thing we were all searching for, and it looks like it could be on a flag or a religious symbol. It was originally going to be grey, but to go with his costume they made it coppery and it looks great.

Frank Victoria, Weta Workshop Designer

DWALIN

COSTUME, HAIR AND MAKE-UP

We were doing camera tests on the various Dwarves in their costumes and all the crew members were picking favourites. It was like a parade of Dwarf beauty contest contestants. The writers have been clever in cultivating varied appeal for each of the Dwarves. They will appeal to all ages of women and possibly all ages of men. There is a Dwarf in there for everyone. Dwalin, for instance, is our soldier.

Being a warrior, he has strong, square shoulders. His fur lends him both a hint of royalty and a savagery.

Ann Maskrey, Costume Designer

Dwalin is a fighter and a badass, so to me that meant he should look tough and dangerous, as if he had been in plenty of scrapes. We had an old scarred cat with chunks missing from his ears and nose, so that's what I did here, with scars going back up into Dwalin's beard and hairline.

Hair and beards are a big deal to Dwarves. With Dwalin being bald, I thought he might have something that was a bit like a replacement for his hair – warding runes or symbols.

We tattooed up Dwalin's hands with shapes that were reminiscent of axe blades. Peter liked the idea of him having runes on his hands and suggested the Dwarven battle cry, 'Axes of the Dwarves! The Dwarves are upon you!'

William Furneaux, Weta Workshop Designer

DWALIN'S WEAPONS AND PROPS

Working in the 3D modelling department this design brief came out of the blue, but basically we needed to come up with some knuckle-dusters for Dwalin. Peter liked the idea of chains that were linked to a wrist strap so that when a fist was pulled the knuckle pieces would stick out and be really nasty. I quickly drew up some variations and we did a test fitting with two of the designs. Peter liked them both, so Dwalin ended up with one of each.

Ed Denton, Weta Workshop 3D Model Maker

AM
CD

ED
WW

ED
WW

AM
CD

MS
AD

JH
AD

GH
WW

We were looking for themes to attach to characters to help the audience discern them easily. For a while one way that manifested was in Dwalin maybe having an animal motif, perhaps a ram or fox. It didn't make it through, but there were some great designs done *(above and below)*.

Dan Hennah, Production Designer

Dwalin's axes were something that appeared right at the beginning of his design phase, when we were trying to find distinctive silhouettes for each of the Dwarves. He was always going to be the fighter, so I put paired axes on his back to give him a unique outline, and it stuck. That led me on to drawing up his axes, which ended up being simple and functional.

Gus Hunter, Weta Workshop Designer

The weapon design process at Weta Workshop was very inclusive. I was able to talk with the designers about what kind of hammer and axes I wanted.

A nice part for me was the notion that Dwalin would name his axes. It's not Tolkien, but I always remembered Emily Brontë had two hounds that she called Grasper and Keeper. She was a tiny little woman, but had these enormous dogs and they struck me as great names. It was just for me to imagine, but I mentioned it to Peter and he said, 'Yeah, yeah, this'll be great. We can engrave them with their names and they'll look really cool!' and now there they are, Emily's axes!

Graham McTavish, Actor, Dwalin

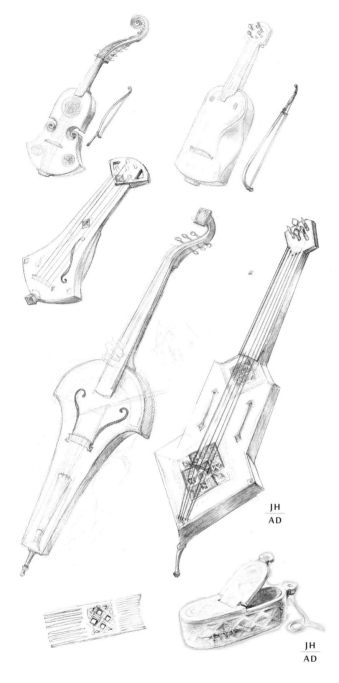

I created concepts for instruments for all the Dwarves, following Tolkien's checklist, even making cases for them to travel in. Ultimately, Peter felt that the idea of them lugging the equivalent of base viols all around Middle-earth was unnecessary, so only Dwalin kept his fiddle. I am fortunate in having a son with a master's degree in Early Music, so have become familiar with the astonishing shapes and sounds of Medieval, Renaissance and Baroque instruments. I do hope he approves of Dwalin's fiddle.

John Howe, Concept Art Director

KILI

KILI'S COSTUME

Kili's costume had to show his royal lineage and yet still look like the young warrior prince. His long coat is made from Dakota leather with a distressed treatment, which gave it life and texture and differentiated it from some of the other leathers used on the Dwarves. It is trimmed with fur and also with a technique we developed of sandwiched laser-cut leather in-between the outer leather exterior and the lining. The Dwarven design on the laser-cut leather shows up in the same way as *trapunto* work and yet is a little more subtle, almost only really showing up in a way that a brass rubbing does.

As a way of linking them, the same technique was used, to a greater extent, on Kili's costume, and on Thorin's gauntlet.

Ann Maskrey, Costume Designer

Aidan Turner, who was cast as Kili, has really fine features. To cover him up with prosthetics just wasn't going to work. We tried subtle prosthetic noses and foreheads to try and square him up, like we imagine a Dwarf might look, but they just kept getting smaller and smaller with every version. Peter, Fran and Philippa really wanted to retain his handsome looks, so the less we put on his face, the better. It was the same story with the tattoos and facial hair.

I spent a lot of time on both him and Fili. Maybe being a girl they thought I'd be a good judge of what's hot and what's not? It was really a learning curve with all the Dwarves and the message was, less is more.

Lindsey Crummett, Weta Workshop Designer

Kili and Fili, being the youngest and handsomest, were our sexy Dwarves, but it was a challenge to keep them that way while still trying to transform them into what people expect a Dwarf to look like. We went through many refinements for Kili. We found that too much prosthetic on his brow risked making him look thuggish, and making his nose bigger could be clownish. He had to be hunky, but fresh-faced. We also made beards for everyone, but it came down to letting him grow his own because it was to be very short.

Peter King, Make-up and Hair Designer

We tried so many hair and face designs for the younger Dwarves, trying to find their characters and not lose the actors' youth, which was tough sometimes because actor Aidan Turner doesn't have a classically Dwarven look. At times it felt like we were pulling against his natural appearance with our earlier designs, but when Aidan joined us a few weeks before the shoot it was instant – we knew Peter, Fran and Philippa had found a great actor we could all believe and trust in as Kili. He was a delightful and gracious person to work with.

Richard Taylor,
Weta Workshop Design & Special Effects Supervisor

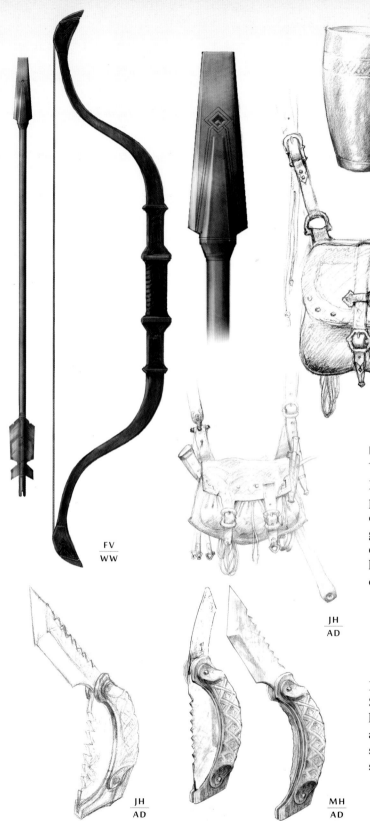

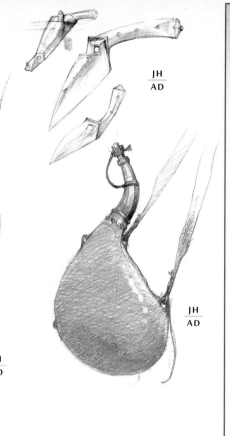

KILI'S WEAPONS AND PROPS

Early on the project, and especially with respect to hero props, the concept artists like Alan Lee and John Howe would do lead drawings, drawing very specific items which would go through the approvals process through Dan Hennah and eventually come back to us designers. We would produce highly detailed drawings or flesh out the concepts to provide drawings to build directly from (*e.g. Kili's peasant knife, left*).

Mat Hunkin, Prop Designer

Folding knives had been around a long time before the Swiss army made them ubiquitous … for millennia they had traditionally been peasant tools: the Romans had them, as did the Vikings, and one was unearthed from the Celtic site of Halstatt. Kili's is practical, as are all things Dwarven, serving both as a knife and a saw.

John Howe, Concept Art Director

DWARF PIPES

Dwarves revere smoking. It is a bit like the German culture in the 20th Century. They had a big thing about smoking pipes and developed very ornate designs. The basic function of a pipe is pretty simple - it is to hold the tobacco and not let it fall apart as it reduces to ash, allowing the user to experience the smoke. The basic principles and amount of tobacco held don't vary much between pipes, but the style of it does. A good pipe might take 20 minutes to smoke if you are working at it. The Dwarves' aesthetic comes through in all their props. It's a slightly art deco feel, so we tried to incorporate that into a smoking apparatus and offering diversity that would help differentiate each character. Some have tall type bowls with long stems, some short; some might be made out of clay while some are rosemary, but in general they are all slightly fanciful. They are an opportunity for the Dwarves to express themselves quite decoratively without sacrificing masculinity.

Dan Hennah, Production Designer

FILI

HAIR AND MAKE-UP

I did a lot of Fili concepts. Given he was a young, handsome Dwarf, we couldn't do much to change his face. We looked at all kinds of variations of hair and beard, plaits and decoration, very intricate to begin with but becoming simpler as we went along.

Gus Hunter, Weta Workshop Designer

GH
WW

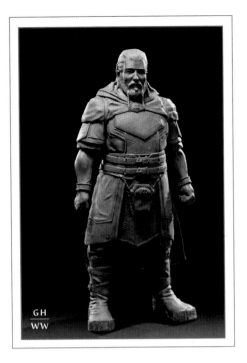

GH
WW

NK
WW

NK
WW

PT
WW

FILI'S PROPS AND WEAPONS

Fili was to be bristling with weapons. They're all over him: little knives, miniature throwing axes, his paired swords, and a war hammer. One of the really interesting things to come out of this concept was the dual scabbard for his swords, which he'd wear across his back, so it made an interesting silhouette. It sits across one shoulder; one is drawn from underneath, the other from over the shoulder, so it's unique, which is what we were going for.

Nick Keller, Weta Workshop Designer

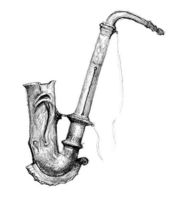

Fili received a full kit, like the others, including a brass pipe with a boar's head forming the bowl and a tall stem at a sharp angle. It also came with a scuffed and worn boiled leather case. Even the dispossessed carry precious objects that they cherish, as well as battered and serviceable items, like this knocked-about lantern.

John Howe, Concept Art Director

Fili was to have lots of small throwing weapons, both knives and axes. I designed the knives for his upper arms, though they were shifted to fit in his vambraces. We also designed a little royal crest *(below)* for the pommel of the dagger I designed. Nick Keller ran with it and it wound up on many of Fili's things, which was fitting, given he's a prince.

Paul Tobin, Weta Workshop Designer

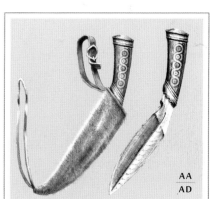

FILI'S THROWING AXES

Throwing axes, or rather axes that can be thrown, always present a difficult prospect, as their rotation must match the distance to a moving target, or the adversary would receive a nasty thump with a handle – and a new weapon to use. I imagined these might 'stick,' so to speak, more easily.

John Howe, Concept Art Director

JH/NK
AD/WW

JH
AD

JH/NK
AD/WW

NK
WW

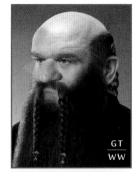

DORI

HAIR AND MAKE-UP

Mark Hadlow is a New Zealand actor with a long and illustrious career. It was a treat to work with him because he is constantly uplifting and always has a funny word. He took so warmly to everything we were developing with him for his character, Dori.

Richard Taylor,
Weta Workshop Design & Special Effects Supervisor

Sometimes a design really helps cement a character and in the case of Dori I think this really happened. I think Dori's final beard design concept *(left)* perhaps helped Mark discover the character because, when he saw this, Dori suddenly became a very fussy person with a wonderful northern accent. It's a very fussy hair do and beard that obviously take him a lot of time and energy to arrange. It's not necessarily practical, but it's great and says a lot about the character in a glance.

Peter King, Make-up and Hair Designer

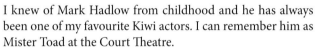

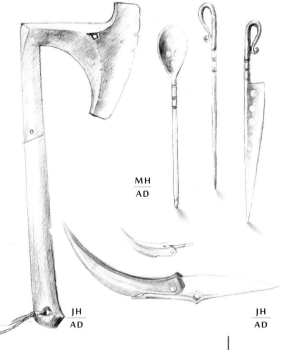

I knew of Mark Hadlow from childhood and he has always been one of my favourite Kiwi actors. I can remember him as Mister Toad at the Court Theatre.

I came up with his beard idea based on the notion that everything Dwarven is so intricate and beautifully crafted. I thought that would carry through to their facial hair, too. It was also intended to be practical because it lifts his beard up, out of the way of tangles when travelling. The intricate weaves and plaiting are all kept close to his face. I wasn't going for fussy, but I can now see it and it works for Dori. It was the only one I did and they picked it straight off.

For his make-up I suggested that his jaw would jut out, and I gave him a bit of a Popeye face that's been whacked a few times.

Johnny Fraser-Allen, Weta Workshop Designer

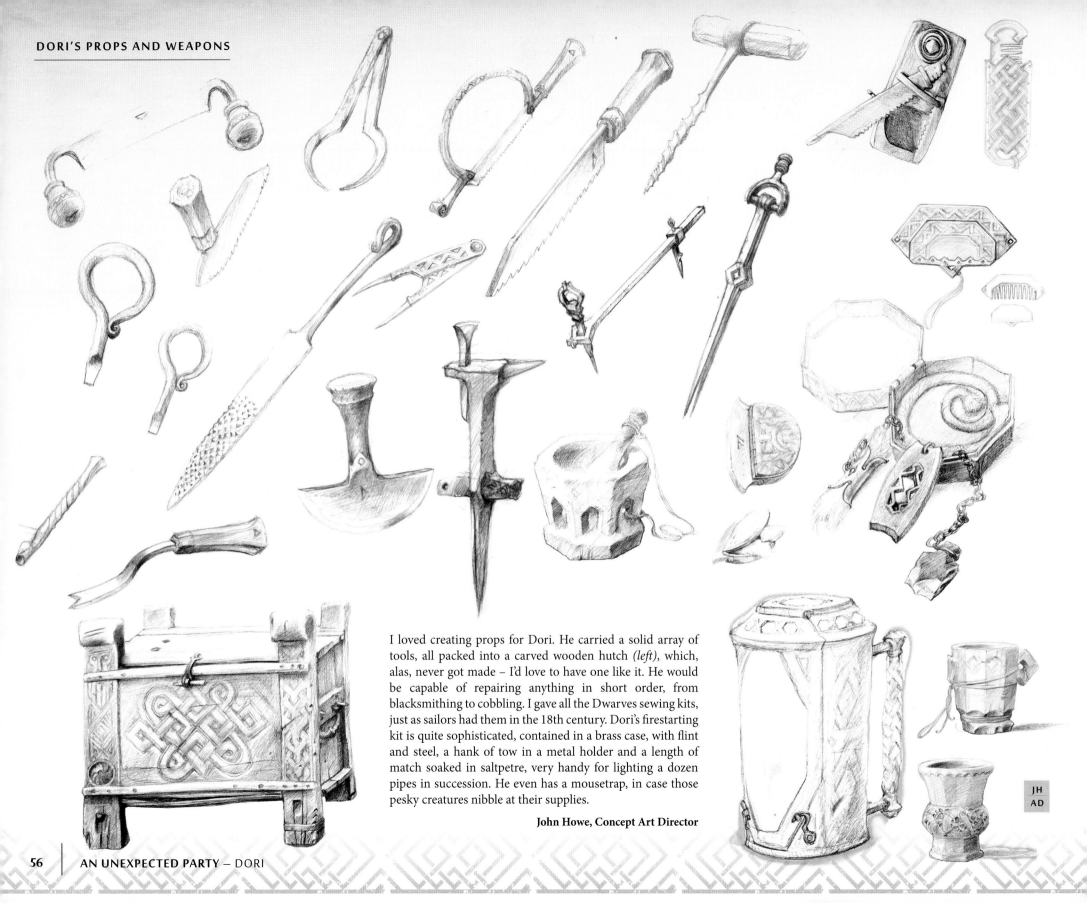

I loved creating props for Dori. He carried a solid array of tools, all packed into a carved wooden hutch *(left)*, which, alas, never got made – I'd love to have one like it. He would be capable of repairing anything in short order, from blacksmithing to cobbling. I gave all the Dwarves sewing kits, just as sailors had them in the 18th century. Dori's firestarting kit is quite sophisticated, contained in a brass case, with flint and steel, a hank of tow in a metal holder and a length of match soaked in saltpetre, very handy for lighting a dozen pipes in succession. He even has a mousetrap, in case those pesky creatures nibble at their supplies.

John Howe, Concept Art Director

JH
AD

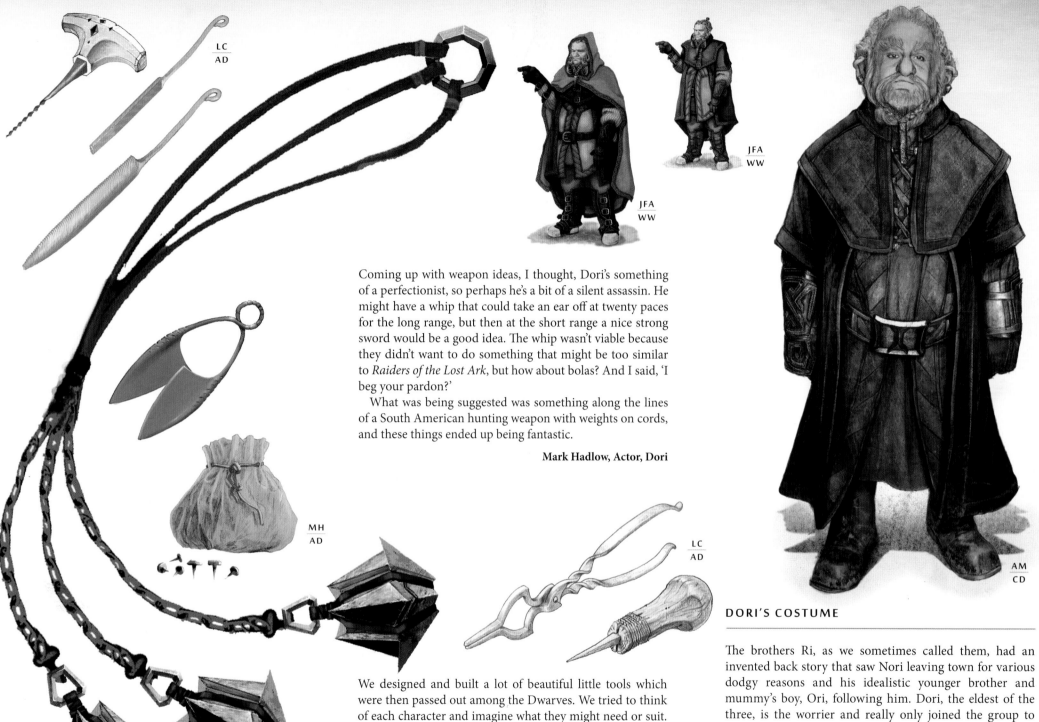

Coming up with weapon ideas, I thought, Dori's something of a perfectionist, so perhaps he's a bit of a silent assassin. He might have a whip that could take an ear off at twenty paces for the long range, but then at the short range a nice strong sword would be a good idea. The whip wasn't viable because they didn't want to do something that might be too similar to *Raiders of the Lost Ark*, but how about bolas? And I said, 'I beg your pardon?'

What was being suggested was something along the lines of a South American hunting weapon with weights on cords, and these things ended up being fantastic.

Mark Hadlow, Actor, Dori

We designed and built a lot of beautiful little tools which were then passed out among the Dwarves. We tried to think of each character and imagine what they might need or suit. There were basic sewing things, jewellery or wood-working tools and the like, but it was all small, hand-held stuff that the Dwarves would carry with them on the road rather than a complete workshop.

Nick Weir, Prop Master

DORI'S COSTUME

The brothers Ri, as we sometimes called them, had an invented back story that saw Nori leaving town for various dodgy reasons and his idealistic younger brother and mummy's boy, Ori, following him. Dori, the eldest of the three, is the worrier and really only joined the group to ensure his youngest brother's safety. He mothers Ori and, reflecting this in his costume, his purple is a bit of an old lady colour. He has a fussy beard in keeping with his fusspot character.

Ann Maskrey, Costume Designer

NORI

It was a great joy to us to see Jed Brophy cast in the role of Nori. We have a long history with Jed and he has always been so supportive of the various creative endeavours we have aspired to get off the ground. Peter really wanted us to have a lot of fun with Nori's look. He's a great character and deserved a very memorable look, and we knew Jed would carry it off with his usual style and charm.

Richard Taylor,
Weta Workshop Design & Special Effects Supervisor

HAIR AND MAKE-UP

I'm probably the guy responsible for Nori's hair so send your mail to me! Peter wanted something very unique, hence the starfish hair-do. Most of the Dwarves were designed by this point and Nori needed something distinctive to go with his quirky character. Greg Tozer came up with the beard.

Paul Tobin, Weta Workshop Designer

NORI'S WEAPONS

Richard Taylor offered us the opportunity to have input into our weapon designs, pairing us with designers to come up with designs together. My primary weapon is a big bongy-knocker-thing, which I thought could be loosely based on a Maori *taiaha* or bladed quarter-staff, in terms of how it should be used, but turned into a more Dwarven looking weapon.

Because Nori has been out on his own, he's picked it up rather than had it handed down to him. It could actually be a mining tool, with one end for breaking rocks out of a rock face and the other to smash them, but also a very effective weapon.

Nori's fleshing knives are based on Nepalese *kukris*, but as imagined through the eyes of a Dwarf weaponsmith. It was a thrill to be able to have input into the kind of weapons I'd love to use.

Jed Brophy, Actor, Nori

The ideas for Nori's weapons came from actor Jed Brophy. We had a big chat and he was a really cool guy with some specific ideas. His staff was the kind of weapon he could use to knock Orcs off their feet. He wanted knives that he could pull out of a double scabbard, and Jed also wanted to have four others hidden around his body so that he'd be one of these characters who was a close combat specialist, with blades that he can pull out of anywhere and stab you.

Gus Hunter, Weta Workshop Designer

AA
AD

JH
AD

GH
WW

GH
WW

PT
WW

PT
WW

GH
WW

ORI

JH/MS
AD

ORI'S GAME

The board game the Dwarves play is based on *gwyddbwyll* or *fidhcheall*, an ancient Celtic game that possibly originated in Wales and Ireland. In the *Mabinogion*, King Arthur and the knight Owain famously play each other.

Like many board games, it is a metaphor for both battle and the perils of kingship, the beleaguered king beginning in the middle of the board, surrounded by his warriors and in turn besieged by the enemy occupying the perimeter. In the Dwarven version, the moves are distantly akin to those of chess, with dice added for fate's turn. A simpler modern equivalent might be fox and hounds.

John Howe, Concept Art Director

ORI'S HAIR AND MAKE-UP

The description we were given for Ori was as a bit of a mummy's boy who's had a very sheltered life, so to me that suggested a bowl cut, something parents give their kids because it's easy. Colour was another thing. His is lavender, which isn't the most masculine of colours and Peter had talked about having a twist of it in his hair.

Beards are everything to Dwarves, so I thought the notion of him having a pretty wispy one would put him in the lower rank and make him seem younger. You see some teenagers who are desperate to grow beards and let this wispy fluff grow under their chins or spend three or four years growing something that almost amounts to a moustache. I thought that would be fun for Ori.

Chris Guise, Weta Workshop Designer

ORI'S WEAPONS AND PROPS

Ori carries an artist's kit. He has a sketchbook which Adam Brown actually did his own drawings in. He was pretty good. The look of the kit went through some changes. It ended up quite simple, with some charcoal sticks and pens and things, less formal than Balin's lawyer-like set up.

Nick Weir, Prop Master

Peter was keen for Ori to have a sling. My father had an old handmade wooden catapult which I brought in for Peter to see. He seemed to like it, so we ended up designing a Dwarf-sized version of my Dad's catapult, which was cool.

Paul Tobin, Weta Workshop Designer

ORI'S COSTUME

Ori was one of the most fun characters to define with costume, in part because Adam embraced it so wholeheartedly. He had to be soft and naive as befitted his back story, so we gave him a number of knitted elements, all a bit cosy. Even his boots were made with round toes. He was in softly quilted lavender, such a contrast to a Dwarf like Dwalin, for example, who was the total soldier. Ori had never left home in his life, but in our story he has run off to join his brother Nori, who's the bad boy who had to leave town. Ori was looking for excitement, while eldest brother Dori has come along to look after him.

Ann Maskrey, Costume Designer

Ori isn't a warrior at all, so he doesn't carry a lot of weapons like some of the Dwarves. He's more focused on his art kit and quills, and documenting the journey they're on with these tools. I had a lot of meetings with the Art Department and learned calligraphy. My quill is my sword.

I recall being in a weapons meeting and the others were all going crazy over their weapons. It was Richard who said to me, 'You should have a slingshot,' and it just kind of stuck.

There's a moment where Ori's very clumsy with it in the beginning, but he becomes quite proficient and even takes on a Troll, whacking a stone straight up his nose.

Adam Brown, Actor, Ori

OIN

OIN'S HAIR, MAKE-UP AND COSTUME

We were all searching for something iconic to pin on our Dwarves that would make them stand out. I thought of maybe one of them having really woolly hair. When I started, I was trying shapes and braids, but then I thought maybe the actual texture of the hair could be a distinctive feature too.

I found some great references for woolly, curly, puffed-out hair that reminded me of sheep's wool. It was in keeping with the theme of Frank Victoria's curled moustache design, which looked like curling ram's horns. The braid was something borrowed from unmarried North African tribesmen. It was originally for Balin but ended up going to Oin.

Lindsey Crummett, Weta Workshop Designer

In the quest for something distinctive, one idea I had was that perhaps Oin was albino *(above, bottom left)*. It didn't fly.

Daniel Falconer, Weta Workshop Designer

There are many different browns in Oin's costume and many different textures in his fabrics. He has a beautiful quilted brown velvet waistcoat underneath his coat, which itself has a certain old man's cardigan flavour to it, and he has a soft scarf. It's the kind of comfortable attire of an older gentleman. I think it's one of our most successful Dwarf costumes because it feels very natural. We'd really worked out our Dwarf mentality by the time we got to this one.

Ann Maskrey, Costume Designer

OIN'S EAR TRUMPET

Researching ear trumpet designs for Oin, who Peter wanted to be hard of hearing, I was surprised to find how beautiful and varied they really are. The prop goes through a lot in the course of the films. It starts out well used but orderly, and ends up getting battered, bashed and even squashed flat.

Alan Lee, Concept Art Director

GLOIN

DF / WW DF / WW GT / WW GT / WW

AL/MH
___
AD

AL
___
AD

GT
___
WW

GLOIN'S LOCKET

Gloin carries a locket with him containing tiny portraits of his son, Gimli, and his wife. There is an exchange with Legolas in which the Elf asks something along the lines of 'Who is this ugly creature?' Gloin indignantly explains it is his wife.

I had done some drawings of Dwarf women's beards that formed the basis of some of the make-up for the film's female Dwarves, which we used for the locket concept art *(top left)*, but I was asked to create the final portraits seen in the actual prop as well *(above)*. For these I looked at the earliest photographs I could find of actor John Rhys-Davies. John played Gimli in the trilogy, so I extrapolated my sketch from his youngest photographs, imagining how he might have appeared at six or seven years old, plus a beard.

Alan Lee, Concept Art Director

GLOIN'S HAIR AND MAKE-UP

Gloin is Gimli's father, so that was a good place to start. As I was coming up with ideas for Gloin's hair and prosthetics I brought in Gimli's colouration and gave him the big brow and nose that Gimli had. Having done that, I thought I needed to individualize him, so that he wasn't just a repeat. I drew some inspiration for a fancy beard and moustache designs from the web. There are websites devoted just to strange facial hair. I saw guys who had put multiple plaits in their beards, but I thought, 'Let's take that a step further and make a curtain of interwoven beard going down his chest with a bunch of little tight braids along his cheeks.' Dwarves are so hairy he could have several of them.

These were all things that differentiated him from the other Dwarves, but there was enough in common with Gimli that anyone who saw *The Lord of the Rings* would recognize this direct link in *The Hobbit*.

Chris Guise, Weta Workshop Designer

CG
___
WW

GLOIN'S COSTUME

I liked the idea that Gloin was a bit of a pack-horse with pouches that would help define his silhouette. My early costume suggestions drew upon Gimli's shapes and patterning, as well as Chris Guise's beard design.

Paul Tobin, Weta Workshop Designer

Gloin was the first Dwarf we began working with. Initially, giving birth to these characters was actually quite difficult, especially because they would be living and performing in these costumes for so many months. There were so many practical challenges in addition to finding their specific looks. Gloin, given his visual links to Gimli, was a good place to start and that's where he gets his colours from.

Oin and Gloin are also brothers. They're the money behind the operation and Gloin has kept an eye on the Dwarves' finances, so there is a hint of this position in his costume.

Ann Maskrey, Costume Designer

BIFUR

BIFUR'S HAIR AND MAKE-UP

When William Kircher came in he told us that when he grew his beard it came through really black and white. Obviously this was the way to go for Bifur, so I just went crazy. Peter suggested that we make a plait of black and white strips of hair. I threw on Keith Richards' hair, from the Rolling Stones, and he said, 'Great! Now let's put an axe in his head!'

Frank Victoria, Weta Workshop Designer

BIFUR'S WEAPONS AND PROPS

Someone walked in the door one day and said, 'Toys,' and then walked out. In one of these mad design rushes I started sketching up concept drawings, but I wondered, were these planned toys or practical jokes the Dwarves were playing on each other, or something else? A couple of hours later we learned these were intricate items the Dwarves would craft on their journey and sell. They are automata or wind-up toys. I did some researching on chip carving and worked up some ideas, one of which was an eagle landing on the Carrock. It was going to be a pillar, but Matt Smith said, 'Why don't you make it the Carrock?' which was a great idea.

Mat Hunkin, Prop Designer

I'd love to relate how Bifur's weapons were based on something clever I came up with. Before we turned up, the designers had Bifur pegged for a boar spear, but they invited us actors in and said, 'We welcome ideas.' So, I did some thinking and came back with the notion of two miner's axes carried on my back to create a good shape, or perhaps I could turn one into a crossbow. They went away and designed all these fantastic ideas which were presented to Peter Jackson, who said, 'How about a boar spear?'

It may not have been my idea, but it's fantastic actually and I have really grown to love it. It has a great outline.

William Kircher, Actor, Bifur

BIFUR'S COSTUME

One thing that had to be borne in mind when designing these costumes and assigning colour was that we didn't overdo their colour theming. While we referenced Tolkien's hood colours, we couldn't make these characters look like they'd been dipped in paint. They'd look like garden gnomes, all primary colours and not natural. No one dresses like that. For Bifur, for example, he couldn't just be yellow. There had to be tones of yellow and then accents in other hues to send it somewhere else. They can't be boring, but they also mustn't jar. I think about colour a lot, trying to ensure we end up with something that looks like it was just thrown on by the Dwarf, but of course it has been thought about and considered very carefully by us.

Bifur was probably one of the last to be designed, but I think he's one of the most successful. There are strong diagonal lines in his beard and we used them in his costume as another way to make him distinctive.

Ann Maskrey, Costume Designer

I spent a lot of time talking with William Kircher when he came in. He was keen to try giving Bifur some mining tools, but when Peter provided his input we started down the huntsman line instead. A boar spear would be something with a big blade that he could brace on the ground and let the animal run right on top of. The prongs would stop it going all the way down to him, but it would still take a special kind of guy to stand his ground in front of a charging boar. Bifur's a bit mad like that, I think.

Paul Tobin, Weta Workshop Designer

BOFUR'S HAIR AND MAKE-UP

We didn't have a brief for Bofur at first. As we started to learn more about him he seemed to be jovial, light-hearted and caring, but could be tough when he needed to be. We started off designing big foreheads and nose prosthetics, but James Nesbitt has such a great face we really needed to be able to see his expressions, so we reduced those with each concept.

One of the first of mine to score a hit had the two braids, which I think it was felt was whimsical and light hearted. With feedback from Fran, we kept the fringe and loosened up the braids. By the time it went through the Make-up and Hair Department he had got those distinctive turned up braid ends, which really helped give him character.

Lindsey Crummett, Weta Workshop Designer

BOFUR'S PROPS AND WEAPONS

It's amazing to draw something and hand it to someone who will make it exquisitely in beautiful, authetic materials. I was at a restaurant and bar one night and bumped into James Nesbitt. He said, 'I love my whistle! But, you know it's too big.' I said, 'Well, it's a Dwarf whistle – they're big.' I was thrilled to hear he was actually going to play it.

Matt Smith, Prop Designer

NK
WW

PT
WW

NK
WW

AM
CD

JH/AA
AD

JH/AA
AD

MS
AD

NK
WW

NK
WW

NK
WW

BOFUR'S HAT

It was fun coming up with so many different suggestions for how Bofur's hat might appear. We were looking for that all-important silhouette again, and he seemed to be developing as one of the more comical characters.

Nick Keller, Weta Workshop Designer

It was good to be able to give each of these Dwarves very distinctive weapons. Everyone coming from watching *The Lord of the Rings* would be expecting Dwarves all to be carrying axes, but in *The Hobbit* we got to expand on all kinds of Dwarven weapons that fit different characters, and that was really cool.

Nick Keller, Weta Workshop Designer

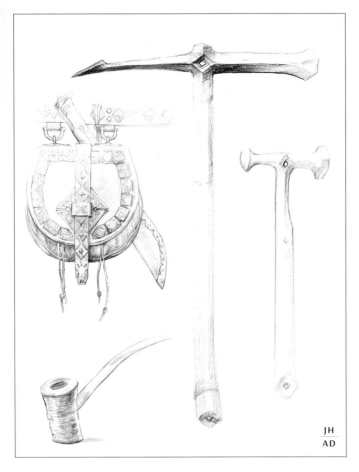

BOFUR'S ACCOUTREMENTS

Bofur was conceived as being a bit precious about his things at one point, so I imagined folding spoons of Medieval inspiration, as well as a lovely glass cup, which of course would have to live in a boiled leather case, complete with lock and a tiny key he would hang about his neck.

John Howe, Concept Art Director

BOMBUR

BOMBUR'S HAIR AND MAKE-UP

One of my earliest beard concepts for Bombur involved him having loads of big decorative metal elements in his beard, but the idea was that these were actually little containers *(opposite, top right)*. They'd look like jewellery but in fact he keeps stuff in there, like nibbles and snacks or valuables.

Greg Tozer, Weta Workshop Designer

I'd drawn so many Dwarf beards by the time I got to Bombur that I was struggling to think of something new. Bombur's silhouette is basically a circle, so I thought I'd go with that as his icon and do a big continuing circle for a beard.

Johnny Fraser-Allen, Weta Workshop Designer

Richard Taylor and the Weta team had begun coming up with Dwarf concepts before I made it to New Zealand again. Bombur's beard was one of those wonderful ideas they had come up with that was genius. We called it 'the strangler' because Peter said it should be like he could actually throw it around someone's neck and strangle them! Bombur's beard is a weapon!

Peter King, Make-up and Hair Designer

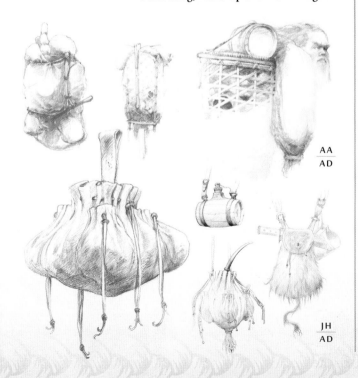

BOMBUR'S PROPS

Everything about Bombur is about food – carrying it in sufficient quantities (enormous), cooking it (in ample cauldrons) and of course eating it. For drinking, I imagined a cup made of the horn of some large cow, cut and capped, with the handle formed over a fire. His knife, while reflecting the Dwarven aesthetic, could conceivably carve straight through a side of … well, pretty much anything.

John Howe, Concept Art Director

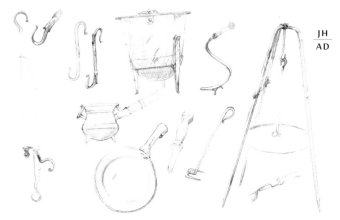

BOMBUR'S KNIVES

Bombur is a man who likes his food so any knife he is carrying needs to be good for preparing food. Function is important in the shape of a blade. Anything that is going to be good for skinning or boning out a beast is going to want a curved blade, while chopping demands a straight blade. There was a lot of fanciful knife design, but in Bombur's case we have erred on the side of practical. Any knife he would use could also be a weapon in a threatening situation. The drop nose blade with the long flat base on it is good for stabbing, but also good for chopping pumpkins, while the curved blade has a little notch for use in opening things. A pointed blade is good for stabbing but also good for boning out a leg of lamb.

Dan Hennah, Production Designer

JH
AD

JH
AD

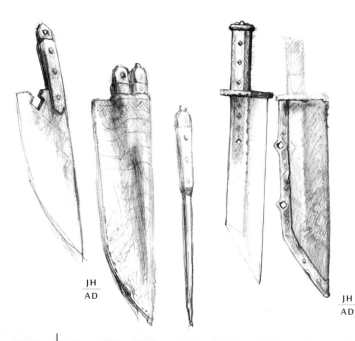

JH
AD

JH
AD

AA
AD

PT
WW

AJB
WW

AM
CD

Dwarven Saddles and Packs

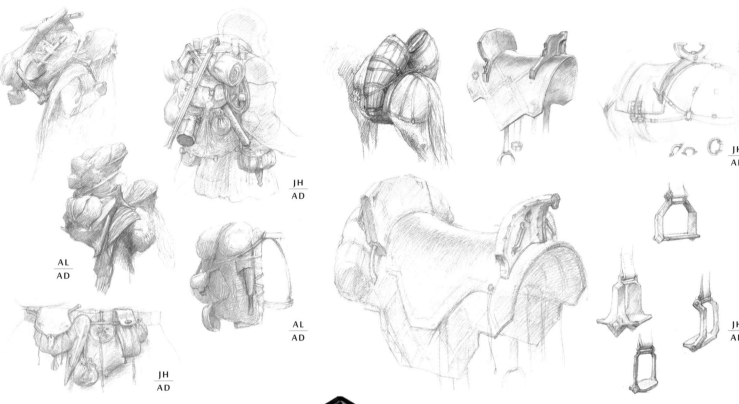

Dwarves are immensely strong (and their ponies equally sturdy), all capable of lugging loads that would have a human on his knees in short order. Because they are on the road and not on a day's outing, their packs should reflect that heteroclite assemblage of possessions. The saddles and pack saddles are based on Viking models.

John Howe, Concept Art Director

The Dwarves' saddles were based on other races' work, but with a Dwarven influence. The Dwarves had acquired and modified them to suit their needs, adding reliable Dwarf-made buckles and fittings. I could never quite imagine a Dwarven saddle shop. This felt like a more appropriate solution, so there are elements of Gondorian or Rohan design in them. We also elected to use enclosed stirrups or pugs. We hadn't done this for any of the other cultures so it was another point of difference.

Nick Weir, Prop Master

DWARVES OF YORE

KINGS AND EXILES

At the unexpected party, Bilbo learns the grim history of Thorin's people and the wrongs they would redress, of how the mountain was lost to Smaug and the humbling of Thror, Thorin's grandfather and Thror's son, Thrain. He hears of the once legendary wealth and skill of the Dwarves of Erebor that drew the dragon from The North and saw their kingdom defiled, of how they were set to wandering. And he learns of how Azog the Defiler took even more from Thorin at the Battle of Azanulbizar, outside the East Gate of Khazad-dûm.

Just as Bilbo does, in these flashbacks the audience would learn how keenly Thorin and his people feel their loss and how hot the resentment runs in his blood. Sung of in Thorin's song, the glory of the Dwarves of yore is revealed and the contrast between this once mighty and prosperous people and the travelling tinkers they have become laid bare. Thorin and the travelling Dwarves, as his company were referred to by the production's crew,

present a picture of a people who are but shadows of their race's former power and wealth.

The design task was to introduce a new supporting cast of Dwarves that would show us what it once was to be Dwarven in Middle-earth before they were laid low and to see what it was that Thorin was so passionate to regain.

The opportunity also afforded the production's designers and concept artists the chance to introduce new Dwarves, very different in look, including Dwarf women, and also see them revisit the established looks of existing characters. Thror, grandfather of Thorin and king under the Mountain in the time of Smaug's coming, was a brooding, resplendent man-mountain of Dwarven power and pride. Dwalin and Balin would appear as younger versions. Young Thorin was revealed, untempered yet by grief and loss, and his father Thrain, heir to the lost realm, was the picture of a leader in his prime.

DWARVES OF EREBOR

DWARF CRAFTSMEN

The Dwarven craftsmen we see at work represent this society at the peak of its culture and craft. We were looking to convey a feeling of a guild so we developed an apron in deep gemstone colours with interlaced strapping that was intended to reference the labyrinthine tunnels and halls of Erebor. Down the side we have runic text that calls out their membership in the guild of silversmiths. It's subtle and ambiguous, but it's in there.

Their shirt fabrics are rich and there is embroidery in their shoulders and sleeves. There's a feeling of wealth and prestige that is appropriate to them as an affluent professional middle class that wears their pride. In talking with Hair and Make-up Designer Peter King we came up with the notion of them having flamboyant hairstyles and beards. It's another way for them to express themselves artistically, so you can see that this is the world that Dori and Nori come from.

Bob Buck, Additional Costume Designer

DWARF MERCHANTS

The Dwarf merchants travel around, selling their amazing creations. They are very wealthy and successful and their arrival is always anticipated. It's very much like the old-world merchants who would go from town to town with wagons full of fabulous fabrics, beguiling villagers. They're their own window dressing in a way, so they wear rich dress and have jewellery and furs, walking billboards for their wares.

Bob Buck, Additional Costume Designer

The Dwarves travel in sturdy carts drawn by curious, outsized creatures. Everything about them says prosperity and solidity, as well as a sure sense of practicality. While there's never any point in re-inventing the wheel, humanity has created incredibly varied wheel designs over the millennia. These construction details were combined with specific Dwarven aesthetics to try to achieve something novel – and still roll, of course.

John Howe, Concept Art Director

DWARF WOMEN AND CHILDREN

Our lovely Dwarf ladies, with their beards and rich, colourful costumes, were a concoction borrowed from the early Renaissance reference, and some lovely early sketches by Alan Lee. In the male dominated world of *The Hobbit* they were a welcome relief, albeit still hairy.

Ann Maskrey, Costume Designer

If you had a beard and you were a woman, you wouldn't just let it grow wild and wiry. I think Dwarf women would be quite stylish, so I did these drawings of it being looped up into elaborate hair styles, along with a slight fifteenth or sixteenth century filter to their costumes.

Alan Lee, Concept Art Director

The Dwarf women and children's hair and beard brief was a lot of fun. I didn't want to fall back on the old 'bearded lady' cliché, so I explored how Dwarven culture might entwine feminine ornamentation with facial hair styling. I wanted the Dwarf women to be beautiful. I also tried to incorporate the already established ornate geometric patterning of their culture into the styles. We've only seen the warrior aspect of the Dwarves before now so it's lovely to illustrate another aspect of their rich history.

Scott Spencer, Weta Workshop Designer

It would have been so easy when designing Dwarf women to make them look foolish or funny, but as these bearded ladies were certainly not being played for cheap laughs in the script, it was of paramount concern to me that we maintain an air of dignity and beauty in them as we set about to decorate our ladies in hair.

The earliest concepts had a lot of facial hair in quiet masculine growth patterns, in reference to Gimli's comment that they might sometimes be mistaken for men *(left, below)*, but as we went along we reduced their beards, placing more emphasis on richly adorned hair-styling that would reinforce their wealth and majesty, and help preserve their femininity. I thought Alan Lee's gentle and playful pencil meanderings among the hairy ladies *(left)* were particularly successful and set the bar high for the rest of us.

Daniel Falconer, Weta Workshop Designer

Some of the designs for the Dwarf ladies went to some pretty radical extremes. We didn't want to go quite as over the top as some of them or as heavy as the early artwork, but we did do some pretty elaborate stuff with jewels and ribbons and extensions. They had to look wealthy and while the idea of facial hair on a woman might be funny to audiences, they aren't supposed to be laughing at them in these scenes.

Nor could we go too heavy with their plaiting or risk them looking like miniature Valkyries.

The balance we found in the end was reached with wigs rather than in drawings. They looked very sweet with little wispy whiskers rather than full beards like men.

Peter King, Hair and Make-up Designer

I have to acknowledge the courageous women among our crew, friends and families who so gracefully consented to allowing our designers to deface their portraits in our efforts to come up with interesting Dwarf lady concepts. There were times I felt a bit like a naughty schoolboy caught drawing hair on the chin of female colleagues with whom I share an office! They were great sports.

Similarly, many of our own children got in on the act. My daughter consented only on the proviso that she would be a Dwarf princess *(right)*. I limited the hair growth to fluff around the cheeks and chin on my concepts to avoid the man-child look. For the toddlers, I thought hats with sewn in hair and ears might perhaps make the exercise even possible.

Daniel Falconer, Weta Workshop Designer

BB
CD

DWARF MINERS

The miners are a hard working, utilitarian folk. Bifur, Bofur and Bombur come from this stock. They clamber like mountain goats up and down cliff faces so we gave them crampons to grasp the rocks as they chip away. It was important to reference the design elements of Dwarven culture that had been established in the hero Dwarves, so there is stamping and stitch work, but they're very leathery, rustic and dirty.

Their little mining hats changed a bit. Peter liked the idea of their candle lights maybe being on the side so they didn't look as contemporary and we made some using pieces cast from goat's horns, which is a nice bit of symbolism considering how they climb about.

Bob Buck, Additional Costume Designer

BATTLE OF AZANULBIZAR

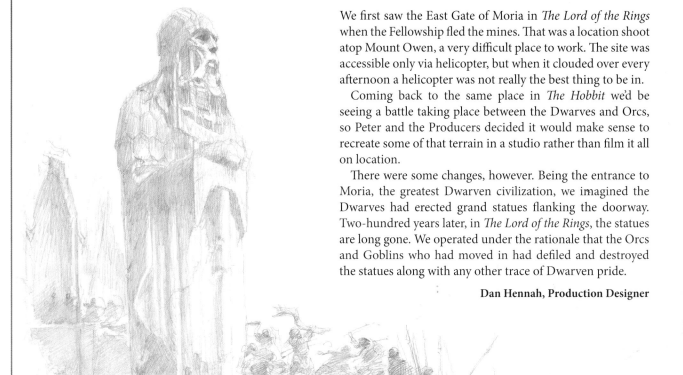

AL
AD

We first saw the East Gate of Moria in *The Lord of the Rings* when the Fellowship fled the mines. That was a location shoot atop Mount Owen, a very difficult place to work. The site was accessible only via helicopter, but when it clouded over every afternoon a helicopter was not really the best thing to be in.

Coming back to the same place in *The Hobbit* we'd be seeing a battle taking place between the Dwarves and Orcs, so Peter and the Producers decided it would make sense to recreate some of that terrain in a studio rather than film it all on location.

There were some changes, however. Being the entrance to Moria, the greatest Dwarven civilization, we imagined the Dwarves had erected grand statues flanking the doorway. Two-hundred years later, in *The Lord of the Rings*, the statues are long gone. We operated under the rationale that the Orcs and Goblins who had moved in had defiled and destroyed the statues along with any other trace of Dwarven pride.

Dan Hennah, Production Designer

GH
WW

In Thorin's past, there is this big battle outside the East Gate of Moria, a place we visited in the trilogy. We had an existing location with very distinctive big rocks to match, so I worked with reference images for the big wide shots, tying them together and painting massive hordes of soldiers like little ants crawling over them *(below)*.

For closer action scenes the focus was on the mood and colour, with fighting and chaos everywhere. The gate is in the background to help remind us where we are, but this is all about the chaos of battle and trying to depict dynamic action *(right)*.

Gus Hunter, Weta Workshop Designer

MORIA DWARVES

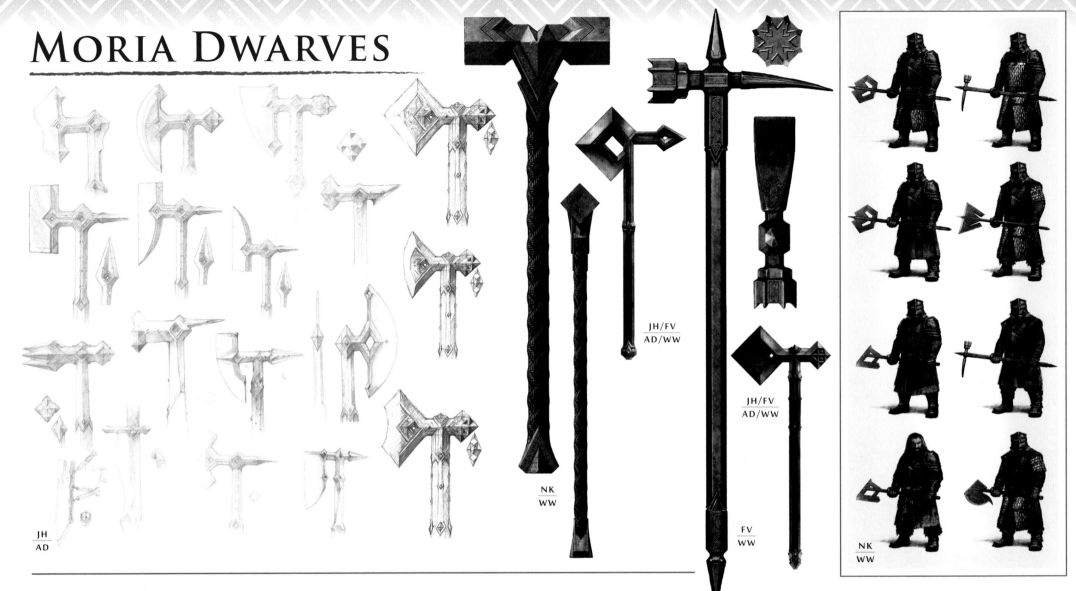

JH
AD

NK
WW

JH/FV
AD/WW

JH/FV
AD/WW

FV
WW

NK
WW

A design process is a winding path with sudden changes of direction and unexpected insights. Occasionally a spark of an idea will appear which will ultimately become the defining element of a design. The pierced diamond shapes in the Dwarven weapons and tools create a family of related objects that are all different, but of the same culture. Once this has been established, then the truly creative process involves creating all the varied versions you might find in real life.

I truly believe that Peter will change how the public perceives Dwarves. Elves, in the public mind, are far different today than they were before *The Lord of the Rings* was published. Tolkien's vision of them has changed them forever, adding a

dimension, or restoring a mythology harking back beyond fairy tale and the Victorian era to the *Tuatha dé Danaan* and the Elves of the Nine Norse Worlds.

Peter is firmly on course to do this for Dwarves. (Tolkien began it by preferring the plural spelling 'Dwarves' to the accepted 'Dwarfs'.) Peter is, for the first time in cinema history, establishing a complete culture and a history, a presence they have never been accorded to date. Thorin's enforced wandering, their memories of glory past and their stirring and nostalgic ballads make them a people apart and entire. This is not the pleasant world of *Snow White*; it's far older than the *Nibelungen*. Dwarves will never be the same.

John Howe, Concept Art Director

The Moria Dwarves were a set of characters I was so keen to get into when I knew that we were going to work on this movie. They're these little battle tanks of soldiers. Though short in stature, Peter wanted them to be immediately recognizable as a formidable force to be reckoned with.

Richard Taylor,
Weta Workshop Design & Special Effects Supervisor

We explored options for swapping parts in and out in different combinations and trying different weapons. While they are an army, not every soldier would look the same.

Nick Keller, Weta Workshop Designer

Originally designed to be the Iron Hill Dwarf armour, this suit was one of the first to be designed, approved and built, though we re-appropriated it for Moria, which was great because it meant we got to do something else for the Iron Hills. The colour had to change a little, but otherwise it's pretty true to what we built. The shapes have the angularity that we have come to associate with Dwarves and the helmet is similar in general shape to Gimli's.

Once we had a general look, we split it out and broke it down into individually designed components, including weapons. We gave them mattocks and different hammers.

Nick Keller, Weta Workshop Designer

THRAIN

With so many Dwarves in the movies, any distinctive features we can pin on a character to help the audience recognize them is going to help. Thorin's father, Thrain, was to have an eye patch upon which I suggested he might have Durin's heraldry, given his lineage. A bold tattoo was also something Peter really wanted, and he reacted well to the suggestion of a beard that was heavily contrasted with streaks of white and black.

Daniel Falconer, Weta Workshop Designer

Thrain's Red Axe was a fascinating challenge. While Dwarven taste favours straight lines and well-defined angles over curves, I wondered if a fierce departure from those rules might not make the axe more interesting. Rules are made to be broken, or in this case, curved. The result ended up being quite radical, but in theory still a wholly functional weapon.

John Howe, Concept Art Director

FV / WW

JH / AD

NK / WW

BB / CD

A giant red hammer with a spike on the end – it's an interesting thing designing Dwarf weapons. They tended to get bigger and bigger, which isn't necessarily realistic from a historical point of view, but they have to be big to look impressive on screen, especially when you remember the Dwarves are actually little guys.

Nick Keller, Weta Workshop Designer

NK / WW

Thrain was described to us as more of a councillor, a reference that influenced the design in terms of his robes. We had him in full-length robes initially, but shortened them to leave that for his father, Thror, the king, creating a hierarchy in hem length. We wanted elements of grandeur and tried to give him breadth. Red was emerging as a colour theme for him, so we adopted that.

I had an idea of trying a mantel of richly embroidered metalwork and tried to develop a kind of Dwarven version of sumptuous matador embroidery. My thought was to put that over the fur and collar so it would be like a symbol of office, somewhat akin to mayoral chains.

Bob Buck, Additional Costume Designer

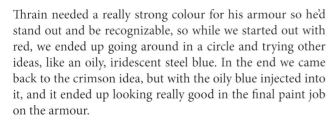

Thrain needed a really strong colour for his armour so he'd stand out and be recognizable, so while we started out with red, we ended up going around in a circle and trying other ideas, like an oily, iridescent steel blue. In the end we came back to the crimson idea, but with the oily blue injected into it, and it ended up looking really good in the final paint job on the armour.

Nick Keller, Weta Workshop Designer

NK
WW

THROR

HAIR, MAKE-UP AND COSTUME

The Dwarves were well established by this stage so I tried to carry many of the motifs that the guys were working into their designs into my Thror concepts. I gave him strong angles and shadowed his eyes under a heavy brow so that there was a certain Dwarven heaviness – a seriousness, weariness and weight to him. I offered some crown ideas. There was, at the time, a strong ram motif coming through that was being linked with Thorin and his family, though that would later change, but it is present in one of the crowns options *(left, top)*.

Ben Mauro, Weta Workshop Designer

BM
WW

Thror's forefathers have all been called the Longbeards, so he had to have a long beard, right? I had the notion that he'd have this big, ornately trimmed beard that would cascade down his chest like a mantle, or perhaps an avalanche of hair on this dark and brooding presence of a man. To me he had to be the ultimate embodiment of Dwarven power and pride.

Daniel Falconer, Weta Workshop Designer

FV
WW

PT
WW

PT
WW

DF
WW

My concept for Thror was that he was an embodiment of the Lonely Mountain, this grim-faced old king who is slouched heavily in his throne and looks like a Dwarven man-mountain. Everything about him, the cut of his fur and fall of his cloth, is all leading the eye up to the jagged peak of his crown atop his head. The triangular decorative shapes in his beard are all based on mountain shapes, something which I thought could be repeated in the quasi-armour shapes of his lower costume. This would be a Dwarf with an uncompromising will, power and arrogance.

The raven crown came a little later once that began to emerge as the dominant theme for Thror's house.

Paul Tobin, Weta Workshop Designer

PT
WW

PT
WW

Thror's dark, mountainous look was established in concept art from Weta, but as we got into it we removed the red and made him all about gold. There's a huge ingot of it on his chest, an armoured chest plate which symbolizes his obsession with gold. We built as much breadth into the costume as possible to portray him as a monolithic king, a personification of the mountain itself.

Bob Buck, Additional Costume Designer

BB
CD

NK
WW

NK
WW

NK
WW

We looked at what we might be able to repurpose from the existing Moria armour, which at this time had been built, for Thror's suit at the Battle of Moria. I had a go at some passes using existing elements recoloured or with added components, some fur and a crown. We also explored some options for giving him a very distinctive helmet with a unique crest, some of which I really liked.

We also ended up establishing a recurring raven motif for Thorin and his family which came through on Thror. We had tried some other motifs, like the ram or boar, even a dragon at one point, though that seemed a bit counterintuitive. Given their strong association with Erebor, the raven seemed the most appropriate.

Nick Keller, Weta Workshop Designer

YOUNG THORIN

We see Thorin as a young prince in a time before Smaug's coming. Initially we offered suggestions that were quite princely, but it became clear that Peter, Fran and Philippa really wanted him to contrast with the pompous grandeur of the scene and be much more of an understated hero. My immediate reference of choice for that was Aragorn. I worked up ideas to suggest he's just come back from a hunt and is dressed in functional leathers.

It's interesting that little things like shortening his hair and tunic, or raising his crotch-line, all help make Thorin look younger: little tricks that help convey a sense of youth.

Paul Tobin, Weta Workshop Designer

Young Thorin's costume for the flashback scenes had to show several stages of deterioration, progressing from a young prince to fighting in his armour, exiled and travelling, and finally working at an anvil. He sheds pieces as his journey continues and what he is left with is very little. The textile breakdown had to reflect the journey and passage of time, but still have the same costume components he began with

Ann Maskrey, Costume Designer

Thorin was to wear a full suit of Dwarven armour. We began by elaborating on the standard soldier's suit *(opposite, bottom left)*, but he became less armoured as the concepts developed. Peter, Fran and Philippa wanted more of a wild man, suggesting he'd been on the road a long time, so less armour and bit more ragged *(opposite, right)*.

Nick Keller, Weta Workshop Designer

Before he ended up in a shirt I was asked to create an image of a sweat-covered, hunky younger Thorin at work at his anvil *(above)*. I think this one was for the ladies.

Gus Hunter, Weta Workshop Designer

YOUNG BALIN AND DWALIN

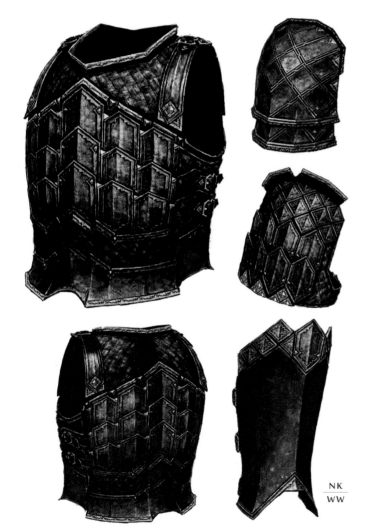

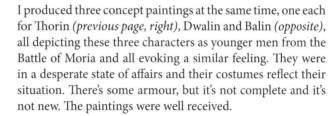

I produced three concept paintings at the same time, one each for Thorin (*previous page, right*), Dwalin and Balin (*opposite*), all depicting these three characters as younger men from the Battle of Moria and all evoking a similar feeling. They were in a desperate state of affairs and their costumes reflect their situation. There's some armour, but it's not complete and it's not new. The paintings were well received.

Nick Keller, Weta Workshop Designer

Young Balin is a counsellor and advisor. He is learned, so I wanted his costume to have a scholarly flavour. His interest in language and storytelling is expressed in the runic elements that run through his embroidery. Simplicity of form with ornate detail seems to be something iconic to Dwarves, but with each character I think we have to contrast that simplicity with a statement about their personality. In Balin, that is his sash, which immediately suggests a scholar or speaker in a forum.

Bob Buck, Additional Costume Designer

STILL IN BUSINESS

THE ORDER (AND DISORDER) OF WIZARDS

Though the heroes might have their own reasons for embarking on their quests, the true orchestrators of Middle-earth fate are the Wizards, and chief among them, though not over them, was Gandalf. The grey wizard would be guide to Frodo and Aragorn in *The Lord of the Rings* and seemingly the only being in Middle-earth to see the grander picture, taking it upon himself to marshal the peoples of its many corners to stand together against the growing darkness.

So too in *The Hobbit*, it was Gandalf who arranged for Bilbo to join Thorin's quest, who indeed orchestrated the quest to begin with, and whose prescience and actions enabled the Company to survive a number of the calamities that befell them.

Played once again by Sir Ian McKellen, the Gandalf that audiences would see return in *The Hobbit* was the same grandfatherly curmudgeon from *The Fellowship of the Ring*, too soon taken by the Balrog, but he would be joined by two others of his order, each representing polar opposites of what a wizard might be.

Saruman the White, head of the order, would of course be similarly familiar to anyone who had watched the trilogy. Proud, unyielding and flawed, Sir Christopher Lee's Saruman was not yet the fallen wizard turned enemy of the trilogy, but in his arrogance and avarice nonetheless might display hints at what was to become of him in the years that followed.

Appearing for the first time was Radagast the Brown, guardian and advocate of Middle-earth's animals and flora, portrayed with eccentric genius by Sylvester McCoy. It would be from Radagast that Gandalf would learn what was transpiring in Greenwood the Great, where the humble wizard dwelt in a home every bit as whimsical and enchanting as his own ramshackle appearance.

The production's art teams would take obvious delight in the contrasting character of each wizard and great pleasure in expressing these differences in their designs and creations, with Radagast and his home being favourites to many among the crew that worked long hours to create them.

PHOTOGRAPH (LEFT) BY TODD EYRE

GANDALF

Gandalf's costume is essentially the same as Ngila Dickson's design from *The Lord of the Rings*, but with a few little differences. Peter wanted him to have a magical scarf, so we created one with a subtle pattern with silver twinkle woven through. It really was quite pretty.

He has a new bag and his boots have changed slightly, plus we trimmed a wedge out of his costume to make it a little lighter to wear, though no one would know unless they stretched out the hem and compared them.

Ann Maskrey, Costume Designer

AA
AD

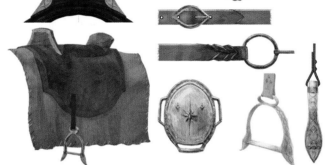

MH
AD

JH
AD

AL
AD

AL
AD

Nick Weir has a good knowledge of saddles and has worked with horses. I've never been on a horse in my adult life, so it was a massive learning curve when it came to designing them for *The Hobbit*, but we had people like Nick to guide the process. We would draw saddles based on our research and get feedback as we went.

Mat Hunkin, Prop Designer

AM
CD

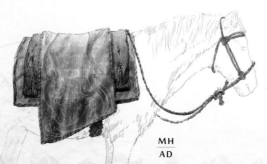

MH
AD

Gandalf begins *The Hobbit* with a different staff. The idea was to play on his association with fire, given he wields the Ring of Fire. The outside of the staff is darker and rough, while the whitish heartwood core is carved in a way that recalls Gandalf the White's. It glows when the staff lights up and creates a wavering heat haze that makes it almost look like flame turned to wood.

Alan Lee, Concept Art Director

SARUMAN

PT
WW

We all chipped in and had a lot of fun developing ideas for Radagast. One of my slightly more out-there ideas had him very hunched and you get the impression he could almost go down to all fours quite comfortably like an animal. He's got birds living on his back like a rhinoceros *(above, right)*.

Paul Tobin, Weta Workshop Designer

Radagast was an open brief when we started and I think you can tell we were enjoying it. Peter really liked the asymmetrical beard idea. We were told there would be a portion of budget allotted to digital creatures crawling around him, so I started working on nests and matted hair that was so infested that it was full of twigs and animal crud and tangled by their activity and burrowing.

Johnny Fraser-Allen, Weta Workshop Designer

AM
CD

Saruman had much the same costume, make-up and staff as he did when we first met him in *The Lord of the Rings*. We made the staff a bit lighter, but superficially it's the same staff. There was no reason to change it.

Nick Weir, Prop Master

RADAGAST

MAKE-UP, HAIR AND COSTUME

Peter's vision for Radagast was absolute genius. He was insistent that Radagast be asymmetrical so he'd literally have one eyebrow up and one down, half a moustache going out one way, the other half drooping down, and a bird's nest in his hair with the birds' business caked all down one side of his face. He's a total contrast to Saruman.

Peter King, Make-up and Hair Designer

JFA
WW

JFA
WW

Radagast's was undoubtedly my favourite costume. I knew Sylvester McCoy from another movie I had designed, and thought he was perfect for the role.

We produced nearly all of Radagast's fabrics within the workroom, either from scratch or by treating existing fabrics to specialist techniques. When complete the costume had drawn on the skills of the whole department with the exception of perhaps the sculptors: dyers, textile artists, the breakdown team, our embroiderer, the machinists and hand sewers, our milliner – everyone. I think he is going to be everyone's favourite character. Serious people will secretly love him too.

Ann Maskrey, Costume Designer

Radagast has a wonderful relationship with animals. I think he's more comfortable talking to them than people. And they completely accept him, even move in. I love the fact that he's got a nest in his hair and the birds nest there and poo over the side!

When I was offered the role I told the filmmakers how I can bird whistle – I talk to birds and they answer! If you know what you're doing, they'll answer with the sentence you've said to them and then try and top it. It's a game and it's great! I was talking to them about that and then suddenly I was bird whistling the script, so perhaps that was where the idea came from? I can't be sure, of course, but the lovely thing was that I had all my bird lines in subtitles, so I didn't have to learn any lines for those scenes!

Sylvester McCoy, Actor, Radagast

Each of the wizards is quite different. Radagast is eccentric, whimsical and gentle, and we played with different ideas for his hat and the other things around him that would help convey this eccentricity. Early on it was suggested that he might have animals living around him and on him, with mice nesting in his beard. We looked at perhaps putting a bird's nest in his staff, but Peter liked the idea that they would nest in his hair.

Alan Lee, Concept Art Director

Two of my paintings were based strongly off some sketches that Peter gave us, one exploring the idea that Radagast's wild beard was actually wound round his wrists and would split when he raised his arms out *(inset, top left)*. His robes were once rich and textured but they have faded and worn beyond recognition *(left)*.

Paul Tobin, Weta Workshop Designer

This kind of character just gets my imagination fired up. He had things growing all over him. He's a wonderful mess, a fun character and someone you never want to forget when you see him. I really love him.

Frank Victoria, Weta Workshop Designer

Radagast's hat was something Peter came up with himself. He wanted the quality of the ears in those side pieces that would yield a very different silhouette to Gandalf's.

Ann Maskrey, Costume Designer

Radagast's first designs were somewhat ecclesiastical, but, as he developed more shamanistic elements came in. I originally started drawing him in long robes but Peter liked the idea of having him wear long johns with the lower part of his legs showing. I dabbled with some Eastern influences but the coolie type hat was too suggestive and took over the design. Big hats can also take over the actor and make it difficult to light the face, so they are usually best avoided.

Alan Lee had done a drawing which Peter liked for how worn, aged and tattered he looked *(opposite, right)*. It conveyed a notion of the character but didn't define the costume so I took my design, which Peter liked best, and blended the two images which is what we ended up with. There's incredible detail and layering of techniques and textures in his costume, a huge undertaking.

Sylvester may not remember but he did propose to me during filming.

... I am still waiting for the ring.

Ann Maskrey, Costume Designer

RADAGAST'S SLED

Radagast has a sled that is pulled by rabbits. The final design *(concept model, middle right)* looked like it was built of sticks with a little deck on the back where he'd stand. We went through a few changes in style and colour but the concept was the same.

Nick Weir, Prop Master

AL / AD

AD

MH / AD

AL / AD

AL / AD

RHOSGOBEL

Rhosgobel, Radagast's home, is deep in the Greenwood, a forest that is gradually becoming infected by the Necromancer's evil, and we see him discover this. We knew from the very beginning that this would be a studio forest rather than a location shoot, so we imagined and built it in such a way that it is immaculate from one angle, but as you move round the trees you would find the rot and the decay, with elements of what we later see as Mirkwood creeping in. The fungi, rot and sick colours were established on the back sides of the trees where Radagast would find them, along with dead animals, all representations of the evil spreading from Dol Guldur, the Necromancer's stronghold.

The concept behind the house itself was that when Radagast built it there was a little oak seedling growing by the front door, which he couldn't bear to pluck out. Hundreds of years later, that sapling has grown into a huge tree that has slowly pushed the house apart. Radagast has kept the building together with repairs and additions as it has gradually warped, but always in sympathy with the tree, so over time it has become this wonky, organic structure surrounding the trunk and spreading bows. A conventional house might be built around a tree, but this one has had a tree grow through it.

Dan Hennah, Production Designer

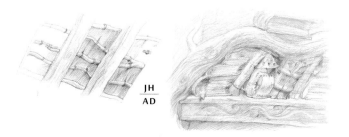

JH
AD

JH
AD

Before we created Radagast's house as a set we had recreated and expanded Hobbiton and Rivendell, both places which were established in the previous movies. Our first foray into a unique set design that wasn't in known territory was Rhosgobel, home of Radagast the Brown. Here we were designing and building the first really unique environment for the films, that paradoxically felt more hobbity than anything that had preceded it, although it's not even in the book.

It's a wonderfully crooked and cock-eyed structure, nudged askew by the roots of the tree that is growing through the very middle and propped up awkwardly. Walking into the final set I thought to myself, we really are finally in *The Hobbit*. Even though Rhosgobel is not in the book, it felt so very familiar. There's something specially intrinsic to this story and Radagast's house embodies that distinction.

The Hobbit is such a different book to *The Lord of the Rings*. Tolkien hadn't yet spent a lot of time wandering the world that was slowly taking shape. It's very rare that a world becomes lighter and simpler with time; they tend to become denser and darker as the author explores them.

The Hobbit differs grandly in tone to *The Lord of the Rings*, a world dominated by the duality of good versus evil. The world of *The Hobbit* is actually a little wider and wilder, danger and refuge can be everywhere and nowhere. There's – as yet – little taking of sides.

Many characters are possibly benevolent but are frightening, such as Beorn, and others who you might expect to be sympathetic but who are actually forbidding and cold, like Thranduil. Friend or foe, and how to know? We are definitely in Wilderland and it's best to tread with care.

Radagast is very clearly on the side of good. He's inoffensive, but he sits comfortably in the wilder world of *The Hobbit*, a reminder that it was originally a children's bedtime tale. It was rewarding to have that slightly lighter, more whimsical touch with him. Nevertheless, he is forgetting the mission of the Istari, so there is a hint of sadness as well.

John Howe, Concept Art Director

ST
AD

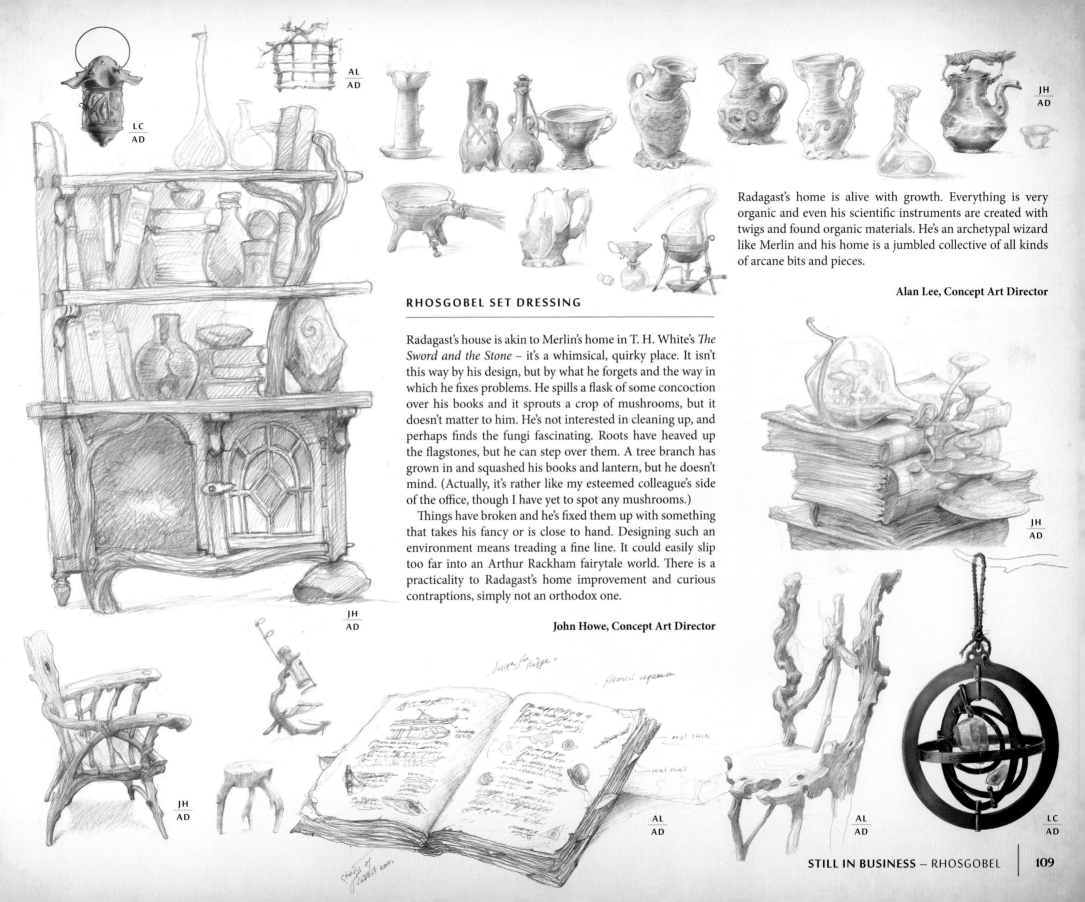

AL/AD

LC/AD

JH/AD

Radagast's home is alive with growth. Everything is very organic and even his scientific instruments are created with twigs and found organic materials. He's an archetypal wizard like Merlin and his home is a jumbled collective of all kinds of arcane bits and pieces.

Alan Lee, Concept Art Director

RHOSGOBEL SET DRESSING

Radagast's house is akin to Merlin's home in T. H. White's *The Sword and the Stone* – it's a whimsical, quirky place. It isn't this way by his design, but by what he forgets and the way in which he fixes problems. He spills a flask of some concoction over his books and it sprouts a crop of mushrooms, but it doesn't matter to him. He's not interested in cleaning up, and perhaps finds the fungi fascinating. Roots have heaved up the flagstones, but he can step over them. A tree branch has grown in and squashed his books and lantern, but he doesn't mind. (Actually, it's rather like my esteemed colleague's side of the office, though I have yet to spot any mushrooms.)

Things have broken and he's fixed them up with something that takes his fancy or is close to hand. Designing such an environment means treading a fine line. It could easily slip too far into an Arthur Rackham fairytale world. There is a practicality to Radagast's home improvement and curious contraptions, simply not an orthodox one.

John Howe, Concept Art Director

JH/AD

JH/AD

AL/AD

AL/AD

LC/AD

WILDERLAND

JOURNEYING ACROSS MIDDLE-EARTH

Middle-earth itself is undoubtedly a starring character in Peter Jackson's adaptations of Tolkien's books on par with any of the heroes. Carrying the analogy further, if New Zealand's landscape was cast in the role by location scouts, it also had its share of make-up and prosthetics, used judiciously to enhance the landscapes' own natural beauty and splendour. These came in the form of digital environments and augmentations by Weta Digital as well as dramatic and breathtaking sets created in the studios and on location by the Art Department.

Finding the character of Middle-earth wasn't simply a matter of flying around with a camera dangling out the side of a helicopter. There are many different environments in Tolkien's world and each has their own flavour and story to tell,

so in addition to scouting locations one of the first steps is the generation of inspirational artwork exploring the environments that characters might find themselves in. This task falls to the conceptual artists and is usually driven by the specific brief of a given environment that serves as the home of a scene, but sometimes there is the opportunity to come up with ideas that aren't necessarily scripted or tied to a known, named space.

For several months during preproduction on *The Hobbit*, designer Gus Hunter was afforded the fun of supplementing the amazing environment designs being created by Concept Art Directors Alan Lee and John Howe and given license to play, coming up with environmental paintings of nonspecific wilderness through which the company might travel on their quest.

GH
WW

MOUNTAINS

Peter wanted to see ideas for some of the country the Company would be crossing as they traversed towards The Lonely Mountain and he asked Gus Hunter to come up with some ideas. Peter wanted dramatic land forms and hazards that would underpin the wildness of Wilderland. There are plenty of opportunities for splendour and equally for peril, even without things like Trolls and Goblins.

Gus produced countless digital paintings of scenarios the Dwarves and Bilbo might encounter on their way, including some really striking mountainous environments.

Richard Taylor,
Weta Workshop Design & Special Effects Supervisor

Middle-earth is huge and varied in its landforms and cover. Peter asked for concepts in which we might see some really different and dramatic terrain. I did a lot of paintings of those. One thing he mentioned was the idea that the travellers might come to a big ravine and they would have to climb down and across fallen trees wedged partway down to get across. It would be very treacherous to try and get over, adding to the feeling of danger and threat that they face.

Gus Hunter, Weta Workshop Designer

Gus is a wonderful landscape artist with a great grasp of form and light, and an innate sense of drama. He portrays fantasy environments believably, suggesting mood and scale in his works. They're a great starting point for defining the character of the landscape. Gus understands light and his lighting will often inspire the digital backgrounds and use of set pieces. He knows how to use these tools to create drama, which is perfect for film concept work.

Dan Hennah, Production Designer

GH
WW

ROAST MUTTON

ENCOUNTERING THE TROLLS

The first hurdle faced by the fledgling Company of Thorin comes in the form of three monstrous Trolls, the very same adventure that Bilbo would later recount to a rapt audience of hobbit children at his eleventy-first birthday in *The Fellowship of the Ring*, and beneath the remnants of which Aragorn and the hobbits would briefly camp during their flight to Rivendell. The difference this time is of course that these Trolls are alive and breathing and very keen to make a midnight snack of the Company and their furry ponies.

The Trolls themselves would be achieved as digital creatures, their design being developed at Weta Workshop and realized by Weta Digital, though the cast would shoot in a set and interact with the imaginary monsters, culminating in a number of the Dwarves ending up on a Troll-built roasting spit. Three of the Dwarf cast, William Kircher (Bifur), Mark Hadlow (Dori) and Peter Hambleton (Gloin) would also assume double duties, providing voices and motion capture reference for the Trolls themselves.

This studio-based Troll camp set was complemented by location shooting to establish the wild lands through which the company is at that time travelling, and another studio shoot in which they would explore the Trolls' hoard, finding therein three legendary swords, Glamdring, Thorin's blade, Orcrist, and the knife that would eventually be named Sting.

In the case of both the Trolls and the weapons, the design task would be a combination of faithful referencing of what went before and clever invention in the interests of freshness and surprise.

TROLLSHAW WILDERNESS

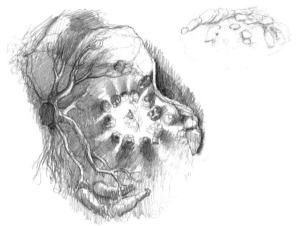

AL
AD

LONE-LANDS

The Dwarves make camp in an area called the Lone-lands. We designed the camp to sit behind a towering rock with a little partial cave in which they could shelter a fire. There's a lonely, craggy old pine over them, but essentially they are shelterless in the middle of nowhere and the pitiful respite that the rock and tree can afford them is all the comfort they can expect in this forsaken place, far from civilization.

Dan Hennah, Production Designer

AL
AD

JH
AD

AL
AD

JH
AD

ABANDONED FARM

Peter wanted to show that the Dwarves were in marginal country, so at one point, shortly before encountering the Trolls, they find an abandoned farm. Originally it was to be that the Trolls had wrecked this house, but later the story became that it had fallen into ruin and been abandoned years ago. This whole area was forsaken by people and was now reverting to an uncomfortable, dangerous place.

Dan Hennah, Production Designer

TROLL CAMP

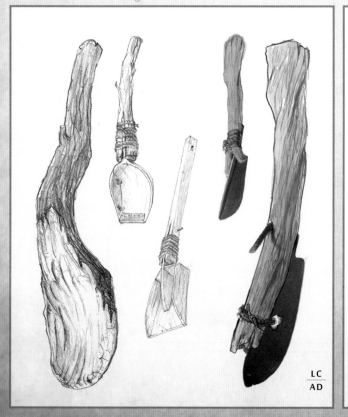

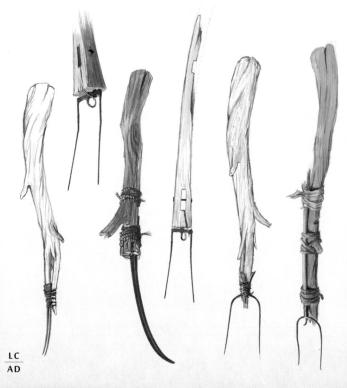

ROASTING SPIT

The roasting spit idea for the Trolls' camp was a bit of fun. The turning spit was a Troll answer to the logistical problem of how many Dwarves can you roast at once and it's a very funny visual. I suspect it wasn't too comfortable to shoot though. You trust that the cast aren't going to be trussed up there and left hanging for too long. Still, I didn't make myself too visible when that was happening.

Alan Lee, Concept Art Director

TROLL PROPS

We took the view that, being scavengers, the Trolls would have kept things from past raids and repurposed to suit their massive size. They don't make their own things. Instead they steal and modify the works of others. For the spit they had rigged up a mill shaft. For a fork, they had grabbed an old pitch fork from a farm they'd ransacked, while a knife was made out of a scythe blade wrapped onto a chunk of wood.

Dan Hennah, Production Designer

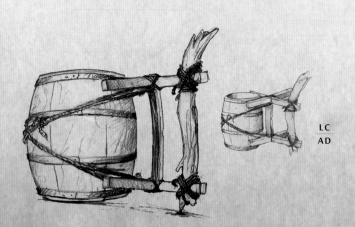

CAMP GEOGRAPHY

Returning to the Trollshaw Forest, we had to pay attention to the fact that we had shot this same environment as an overgrown forest with the Trolls turned to stone. That said, with 60 intervening years, we were able to take some licence and found a really great location that had a sort of primeval, threatening nature that we wanted for the scene.

We needed a rock that Gandalf could break and which would reveal the rising sun across the hollow of the lair, rendering the Trolls immobile. The actual breaking of the stone would be a digital effect, but we had Gandalf standing there atop both full and half-rocks, which we built.

Dan Hennah, Production Designer

AM
CD

DWARVEN UNDERCLOTHING

I had a lot of fun designing the Dwarven underwear. As with all their other costumes they each had a distinct look. Ori had a Dwarven quilted 'Liberty bodice' and very high-waisted long johns. Dori had silk knit combinations with a quilted bib decoration mirroring his shirt detail. Bifur's were the absolute basic all-in one, dyed to an unappealing dirty mustard colour. Nori had very basic grey wool combinations. All the underwear had to look real over the Dwarf bodysuits we had made to distort their human physiques and each Dwarf still kept their boots on. By the time they were all tied to the spit they looked like a bundle of rags, but the underwear does get seen during other sections of the movies.

Ann Maskrey, Costume Designer

AL
AD

TROLLS

We first visited the Trolls in *The Lord of the Rings*, but fortunately, as we never got a really good look at them, it meant we had a little creative freedom to reimagine them for *The Hobbit*. This time they are flesh and blood characters in their own right and Peter wanted to see that reflected in their designs.

Richard Taylor,
Weta Workshop Design & Special Effects Supervisor

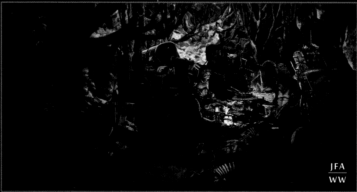

I was in the National History Museum in New York and came across an Asian rhinoceros. I never even knew they existed, but come time to work on the Trolls I just loved the notion of massive neck flaps like rhinos have. Their hide is really thick and plated like an animal. I took inspiration from the original Cave Troll but gave Bert, William and Tom more expressive mouths and more human noses.

Trolls are hoarders, so I thought perhaps when they raided a village or farm they'd jam all this junk and treasure together into makeshift backpack-like contraptions to drag it all back to their cave. I thought maybe they'd live in squalor and be obsessive collectors of stuff so their camp would be like a junk yard, with their backpacks forming their interesting silhouettes.

Johnny Fraser-Allen, Weta Workshop Designer

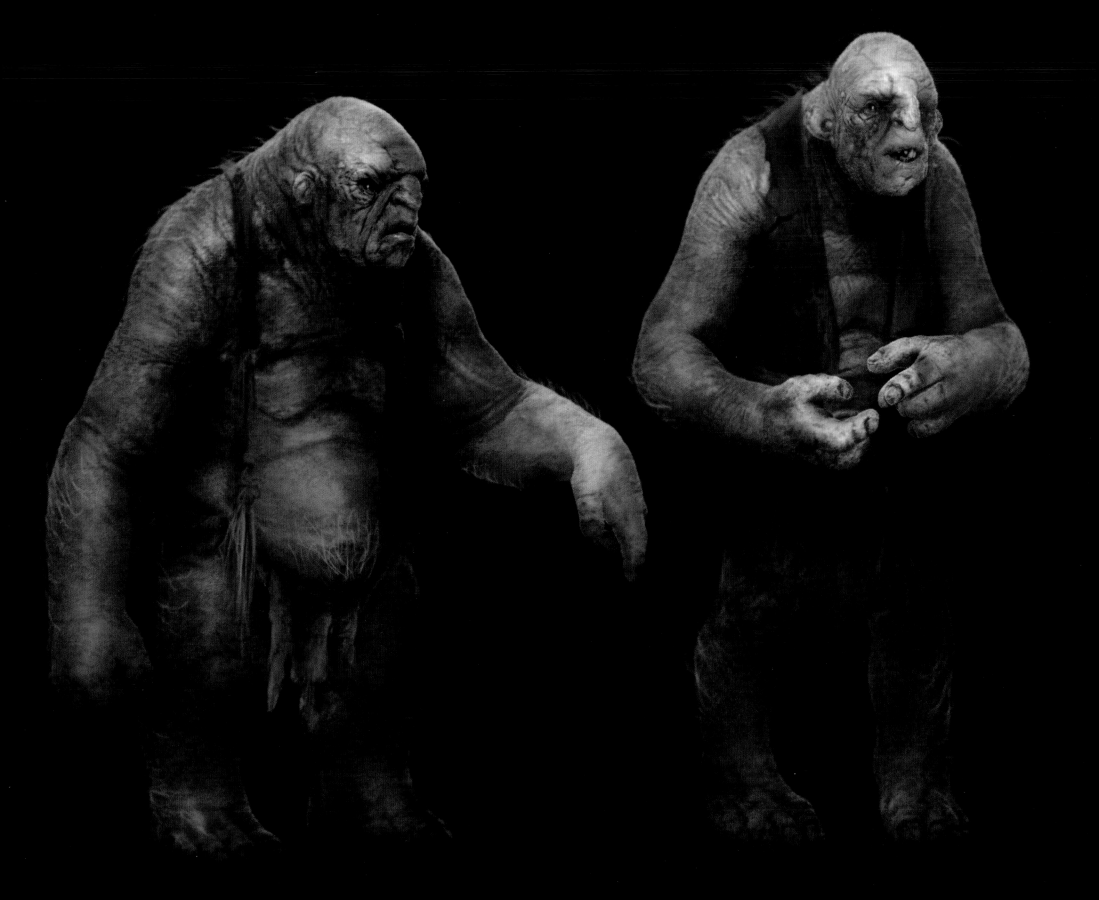

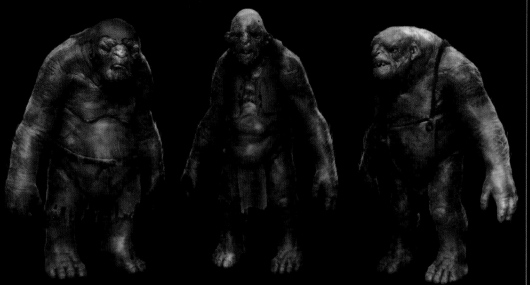

Peter wanted the Trolls to be a little simpler and slightly more human looking than where we went with them initially, as they were going to be speaking quite a bit. It was important, therefore, that we'd be able to read their expressions clearly and the overly knuckled face of something like the Cave Troll might not have suited. So I pulled out my collection of craggy face reference and looked at a wide range of different British comedians and character actors for inspiration.

Peter thought we might try more human skin tones and a fleshier feel for their hides, too, rather than be like all the other types of Trolls we had seen up till now. Always being out at night, I figured they might have paler, softer skin.

In the end, they went through very quickly and were approved with only a few small changes.

Andrew Baker, Weta Workshop Designer

AJB
WW

TROLL HOARD

AL
AD

AL
AD

AL
AD

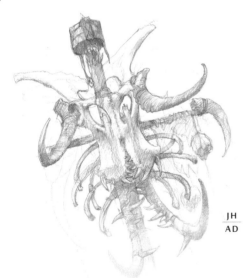

JH
AD

RV
AD

I created a rather horrid last-minute artefact designed for the Trolls' secret cave *(above)*. The script called for 'creepy artefacts … (and) strange totems', that the Trolls might have amassed during their nocturnal foraging. This is the pelvis of a large deer or elk, adorned with horns, teeth and makeshift rib cage, the whole capped by a rusty helmet. The owner has certainly met with a most unsavoury fate.

John Howe, Concept Art Director

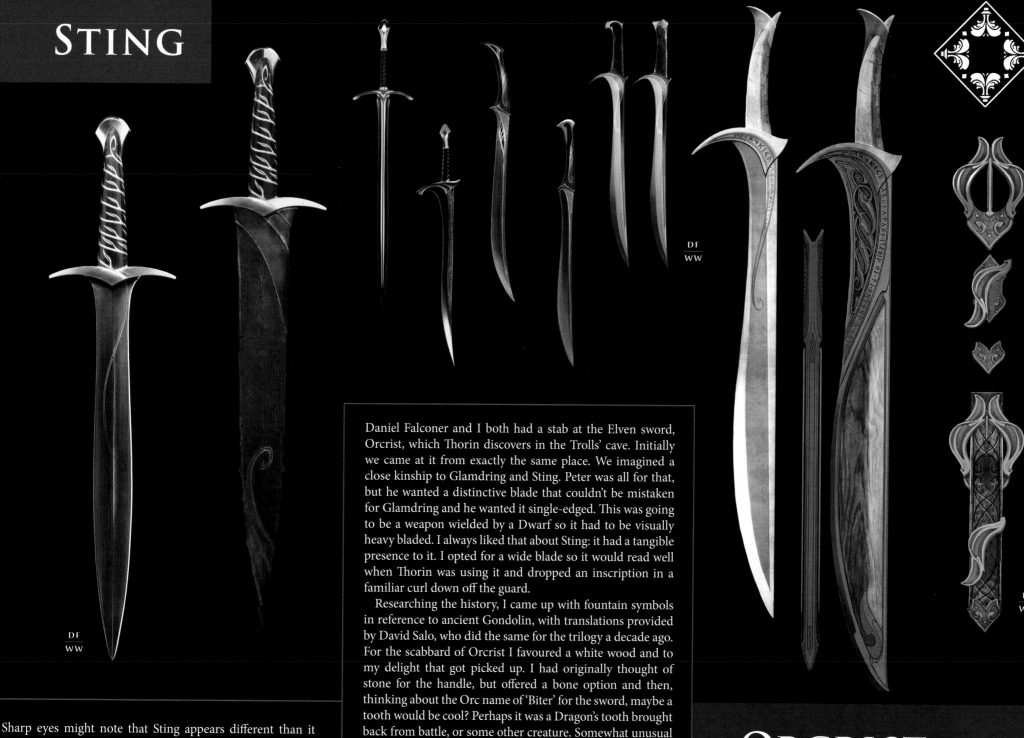

STING

ORCRIST

Daniel Falconer and I both had a stab at the Elven sword, Orcrist, which Thorin discovers in the Trolls' cave. Initially we came at it from exactly the same place. We imagined a close kinship to Glamdring and Sting. Peter was all for that, but he wanted a distinctive blade that couldn't be mistaken for Glamdring and he wanted it single-edged. This was going to be a weapon wielded by a Dwarf so it had to be visually heavy bladed. I always liked that about Sting: it had a tangible presence to it. I opted for a wide blade so it would read well when Thorin was using it and dropped an inscription in a familiar curl down off the guard.

Researching the history, I came up with fountain symbols in reference to ancient Gondolin, with translations provided by David Salo, who did the same for the trilogy a decade ago. For the scabbard of Orcrist I favoured a white wood and to my delight that got picked up. I had originally thought of stone for the handle, but offered a bone option and then, thinking about the Orc name of 'Biter' for the sword, maybe a tooth would be cool? Perhaps it was a Dragon's tooth brought back from battle, or some other creature. Somewhat unusual for an Elf, perhaps, but I thought it an interesting idea and Peter liked it.

Sharp eyes might note that Sting appears different than it did in the trilogy, lacking the inscription which we reasoned Bilbo had added to the blade later, once he'd named it.

Daniel Falconer, Weta Workshop Designer

Paul Tobin, Weta Workshop Designer

A Short Rest

RIVENDELL, THE LAST HOMELY HOUSE

The warding charms of Rivendell and the hospitality of the Elves provide a short respite for the Company on their quest, though not quite the same welcome that Frodo and his companions would enjoy. The Dwarves are much less comfortable than the Fellowship in this Elf haven and indeed the nature of the environment is a little different too.

It is a different time and a different season. The peoples of Middle-earth are not united by a single threat, but much more invested in their own affairs, so Rivendell has yet to become the rallying point that in latter days it would be. Where the members of the fellowship to be accepted the wisdom and welcome of Elrond's halls, the Dwarves of Thorin's Company are mistrustful and wary, looking darkly upon their hosts and being quick to perceive insult or agenda. This called for a subtly shifted presentation of Rivendell.

Additionally, the characters would explore new spaces within Elrond's whimsically sprawling home, including the magical observatory. Though he might resent the help of an Elf Lord, Thorin receives revelations concerning the map he bears, a scene which takes place in one of the dramatic new environments that are visited and for which a new set was designed and built, very different than the other parts of Rivendell seen previously.

For Gandalf too, the short stay in Rivendell brings revelations when the White Council convenes to discuss Thorin's quest and Gandalf's growing suspicion about the rise of the Necromancer. Cate Blanchett makes a welcome return as Galadriel, the enigmatic Elven Lady of Light and Gandalf's greatest ally and confidant.

Sadly the company's sojourn in The Last Homely House is short lived, as the quest beckons and the Dwarves leave swiftly, plunging into the mountains and in so doing leaving behind the last friendly anchorage and familiar territory for followers of *The Lord of the Rings*. Ahead lies wild, unknown country.

RIVENDELL

ARRIVAL IN THE VALLEY

The exact geography of Rivendell was never explicitly defined during *The Lord of the Rings*, but this time we have established an area of Rivendell quite accurately, giving the sets and digital work a common grounding. We also approach it from a new angle, coming down a different face of the valley, so the entrance is totally new.

Dan Hennah, Production Designer

When the Dwarves enter Rivendell it is from a new entrance over a wide bridge and into a courtyard in which they are surrounded by Elven riders. This is one of the many new parts of Rivendell that we see. It had to be obvious this was the same place we saw previously, but we didn't want to repeat any of the familiar vistas. There were other parts designed as well, which we didn't end up making, including a falconery for Elrond's hunting hawks, and a library.

Alan Lee, Concept Art Director

Rivendell as seen through naive hobbit eyes or from beneath furrowed Dwarf brows is a different place than we've seen before. It isn't melancholy, but it isn't necessarily welcoming either. It contrasts sharply with the Dwarves, who are short and hairy, not very clean and have bad manners. They are tunnel dwellers, while Rivendell is bright and full of air and light, a synthesis of nature and constructed buildings.

John Howe, Concept Art Director

RIVENDELL COURTYARD

We cast Rivendell in a new colour palette this time around. Whereas when Frodo visited, Rivendell was autumnal, in keeping with the Elves preparing to leave Middle-earth, at this time we reasoned that the Elves are still enjoying their Midsummer. The colours are more vibrant and inside the fabrics are fuller.

The Dwarves are also very clearly out of their element here. They are awkward and uncomfortable in this space and even end up breaking or pilfering things. At one time there was even the notion of them defiling some pristine and sacred water feature by bathing in it.

Dan Hennah, Production Designer

The Dwarves enter Rivendell across a slender bridge and are all of a sudden surrounded in the courtyard by wheeling Elven riders. I love the scene. They're all so incredibly different, the earthy broad little Dwarves and these haughty, ethereal but dangerous riders, and none of them are human.

John Howe, Concept Art Director

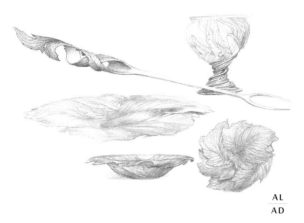

AL
AD

RV
AD

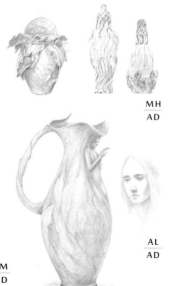

MH
AD

AL
AD

LM
AD

Blues and golds were the dominant colours we employed in Rivendell. Everything was very elegant. The shapes and lines were drawn from nature, but stylized and flattened to become quite simple as opposed to organic like Mirkwood patterning might be, for example. The prints that we used in Rivendell were refined and simplified, pared back to just a few elegant lines, in keeping with the kind of people those Elves are.

Each design was repurposed and applied in different ways, so the same pattern might appear on a table cloth or as a print, but look different each time while still being of one design family.

We also made a lot of poufs: round cushions that the Dwarves sit on. We came up with a shape that we called the pumpkin.

Letty MacPhedran, Soft Furnishing Designer

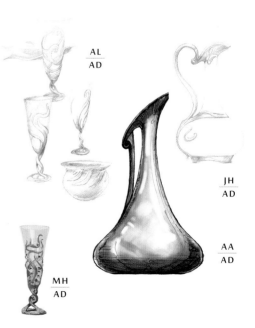

AL
AD

JH
AD

AA
AD

MH
AD

ELVEN MUSICAL INSTRUMENTS

We designed harps and stringed instruments for the Elves, something elegant that they could play with the detached air that they have. The harp is based on an Ancient Greek lyre, but that has been revisited with the Elves' elaborate simplicity, inspired by Art Nouveau. Their furniture is constructed in a similar spirit.

John Howe, Concept Art Director

The lamps for Thranduil's palace and the musical instruments for Rivendell are both perfect examples of the complexity of the props that have been created for these movies. There are over a hundred hand-made components in each prop.

Paul Gray, Prop Making Supervisor

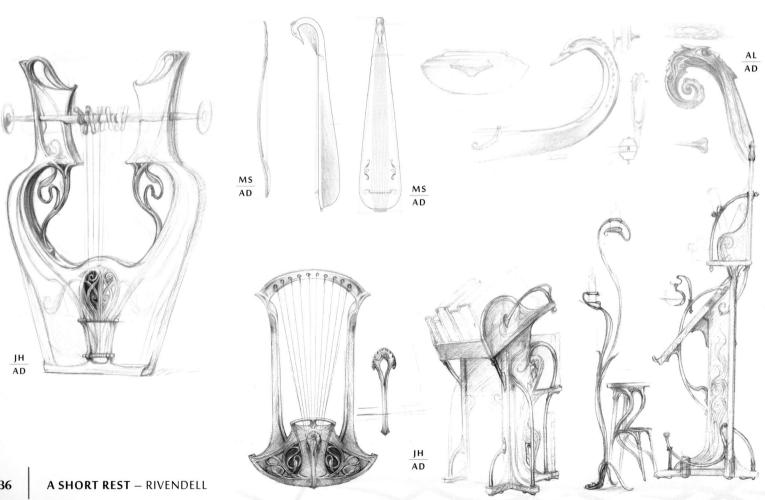

AL / AD

RV / AD

RIVENDELL SLEEPING QUARTERS

The sleeping quarters the Dwarves inhabit in Rivendell was at risk of being monochromatic, I thought. In adding set dressing we brought in some more colour and helped define the architecture's purpose. It's a tapestry gallery. Alan Lee had produced some designs and our soft furnishing department turned them into beautiful, multi-layered tapestries.

Ra Vincent, Set Decorator

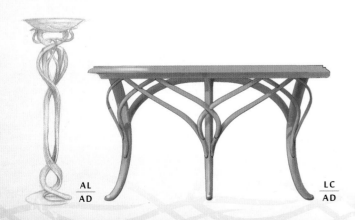

AL / AD

LC / AD

AL / AD

ELROND

For Elrond, I went to silk-braced and cloqué fabric, light and flowing in the way that Elves are, but with a bit of body that could be tailored. The coat is flowing, but the top half is tailored and sharp. I wanted to make him look dignified. We also get to see him in armour again, which is similar to that which he wore last time, but with a new palette and additions.

Ann Maskrey, Costume Designer

RIVENDELL ELVES

There were two distinct groups of Rivendell background artists: courtiers and then servants and musicians. The courtyard group wore cooler, more sombre tones: dark blues, browns and greens, plum and taupe, all subtle shades. They had to look elegant and very much a contrast to the Dwarves.

The men, including Lindir, played by Bret McKenzie, had coats cut in a figure-skimming flattering line, with slim trousers and over-robes. The fabrics were all silks and velvets, soft brocades and cloqués with subtle patterns, and the colours muted yet beautiful and all the fabrics light and flowing.

Ann Maskrey, Costume Designer

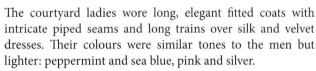

The courtyard ladies wore long, elegant fitted coats with intricate piped seams and long trains over silk and velvet dresses. Their colours were similar tones to the men but lighter: peppermint and sea blue, pink and silver.

The servants and musicians inside the palace wore all golden and bronze shades, which I thought more suitable for the scene. The male servants had slightly shorter fitted coats and the women crushed velvet dresses and simple drapes.

Ann Maskrey, Costume Designer

AM
CD

RIVENDELL GUARDS

Because we were to see Elven riders come in armed with bows and quivers, we designed a rig to be slung from a saddle with a bow that would fit snugly alongside the quiver. In the end we abandoned that because it was better to see the whole bow rather than hide some of it. John Howe had designed a latticework that we adapted for the quiver that looked really nice.

Nick Keller, Weta Workshop Designer

AM
CD

It was suggested that we might make use of the Elven armour last seen in the prologue sequence of *The Lord of the Rings*. Elrond was last seen leading those guys so it did make some sense, even if that was centuries earlier.

Looking for some newness, I proposed that we should try some new colours and detailing in addition to new soft costuming components. We also added to the helmet's brow, removing Gil-galad's sigil. In the end, though the basic pattern remained the same, it was almost a completely new set of armour that we made for the Rivendell guards.

Daniel Falconer, Weta Workshop Designer

The riders were intended to be stripped-back versions of the guardsmen, so my approach was to paint a rider with a few more costumed elements that would help sell the idea *(opposite page)*. Sometimes I prefer to approach colour a little more tentatively in a concept painting because if I pick a strong colour and it is wrong there is the risk that it can be distracting and undermine the design. It can be better to begin monochromatically and work colour options into a painting once the basic design has been approved.

Nick Keller, Weta Workshop Designer

DF
WW

NK
WW

ELROND'S OBSERVATORY

Among the new parts of Rivendell we visit is the observatory, which is a space dedicated to the reading moon runes. We talked at length about how being in this place would allow them to read the hidden runes on Thror's map. It had to be about moonlight, so we designed a space that was built to concentrate and channel moonlight. All around this great crevice waterfall in the mountainside there are statues holding vast polished trays, bouncing and reflecting the light down to a point on a crystal where the moon would be reflected twenty times. This is where the map would be laid. When the moon was just right, the runes could be seen.

It took many incarnations to get to the final design. It had to be something that was clearly understandable in one glance and not require explanation.

Dan Hennah, Production Designer

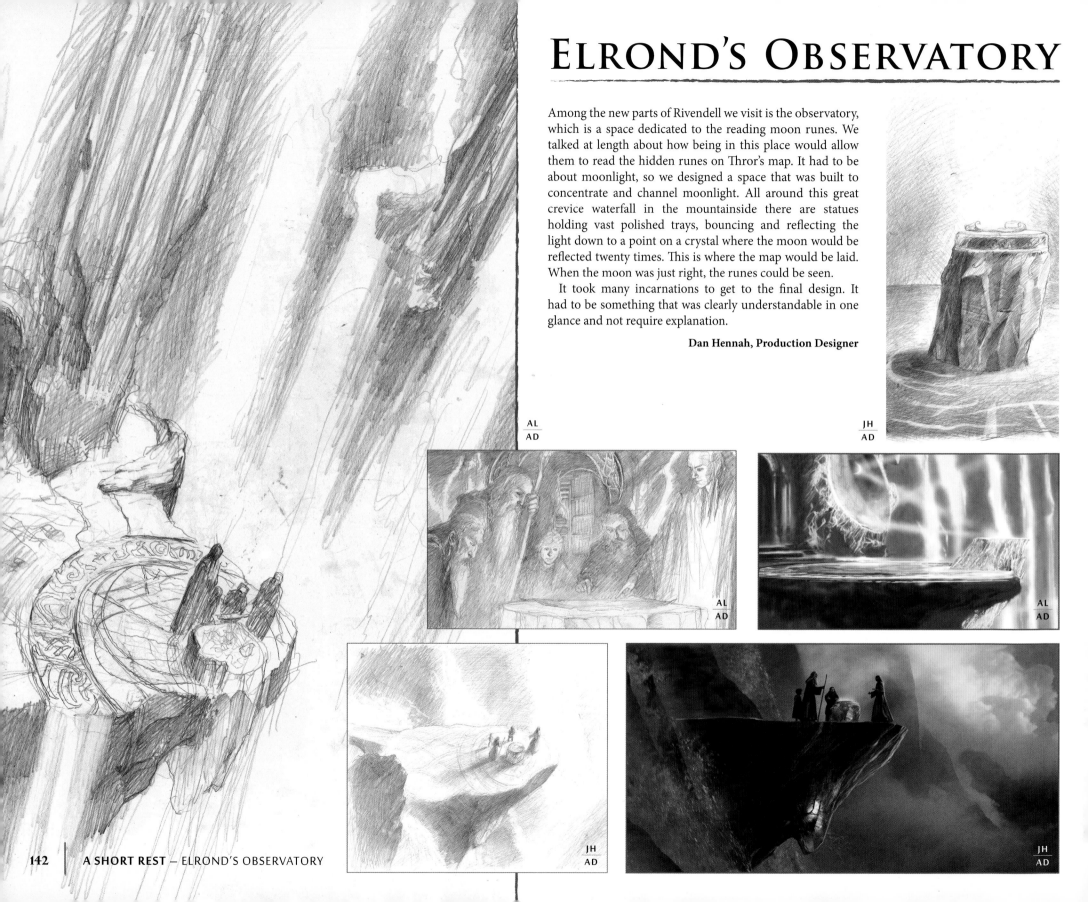

COUNCIL CHAMBER

The Council Chamber was a new environment, but it was similar to the very earliest design we had done for Elrond's Council Chamber in *The Lord of the Rings*, where the formation of the Fellowship was to have taken place before that ended up happening outside. It was a domed, circular structure with a decorative lattice roof and a wall of columns with a commanding view of the valley below. This seemed like a good starting place for this ceremonial space. Inside were sculptural forms of Elven maidens.

Alan Lee, Concept Art Director

GALADRIEL

Galadriel's element is water. When given the chance to come up with costume suggestions for her, it seemed appropriate to base my ideas on water, hence the inspiration for her shimmery Waterfall Dress concept, as I call it *(far left)*.

Daniel Falconer, Weta Workshop Designer

There were many different suggestions put forward for Galadriel. New ideas from Weta Workshop were presented and there was a piece Alan Lee had done which Peter Fran and Philippa liked also. The task was to understand which elements there were in all these things that they wanted to keep and bring them together as a working design. Galadriel was essentially white in the previous movies but we didn't want to make the exact same costume again, or something that was superficially identical. We flirted with adding some colour, like the palest aqua or lilac, but she always came back to white.

In the end her White Council dress was a bias cut silk chiffon with Swarovski crystals hand applied in wavy lines like rivulets of water. The under dress is a silk georgette beaded fabric which ever so slightly shimmers through the silk chiffon top layer.

Her coat was almost the colour of the stone in Rivendell so standing there she had a statuesque quality that was beautiful. Peter had the Art Department add some steps to the set to accommodate the long train of the coat, and Cate Blanchett did a perfect corkscrew turn as she first appears, which enhanced her entrance to the movie and the costume.

In all Galadriel was tricky because she had to relate to how she had been in *The Lord of the Rings* and yet be different, but out of the process I think we created something very beautiful.

Ann Maskrey, Costume Designer

OVER HILL

TOMBS SUNDERED, STONE AND THUNDER

While Gandalf seeks answers beneath the mountains, Thorin tries to lead his company over them, and finds himself at the mercy of elemental forces both natural and not. A storm lashes the heights of the Misty Mountains so powerful and violent that it has awoken Stone Giants, elemental beings who make sport of hurling bus-sized boulders at each other, sending the Dwarves scurrying for shelter.

The precipitous mountain passage, craggy Giants and stone-shattering storm offered fresh design opportunities and the chance to place the main characters in ever more overwhelming peril.

Gandalf's journey of discovery also brought with it the opportunity to explore an environment not visited in the books, but unquestionably Tolkien in nature: the High Fells, tombs of the undead servants of Sauron, the Nazgûl.

In both instances these environments would be realized as a combination of live action studio shooting and digital set creation to convey the necessary scale and atmospheric drama.

AL
AD

High Fells

For my concept for the approach to the High Fells, I wondered if Gandalf might make his way down the cliff, rather than up. Vertigo is so much greater staring down at precarious footing. The top of the zig-zag path to the tombs was signalled by an eerie tilted monolith at the cliff's edge.

John Howe, Concept Art Director

The concept behind the High Fells was that the men of old had taken the defeated nine kings, the Nazgûl, Sauron's chief servants, and sealed their remains in crypts that no one would possibly want to visit. It was no shrine, but rather an indictment, like a prison for the dead.

We found an amazing location during a two-week stint flying around many potential sites in helicopters – this may sound great, but I assure you, you get over it pretty quickly. The pilots had come across this sheer formation in a very rugged valley and Peter said, 'There's the High Fells right there.' Alan Lee then drew a cut vertical face onto the location imagery with an uncomfortably tight path leading up to this tiny entrance.

It is very difficult to access, and then once inside there is a vertical shaft that goes down, seemingly forever. The tunnel is a ramp that would shoot anyone unprepared straight down and into the shaft. Peter said, 'Make it forty-five degrees!' but after we worked out that no one would possibly be able to walk down that incline we looked for a slightly less extreme grade. Radagast and Gandalf had to be able to descend it with difficulty. Some research into the Great Pyramid of Giza turned up the angle of 27 degrees and indeed its main passage was made at that grade for the very same reason. If you were unaware, you would likely slide to your death, so we adopted that angle for our design.

Dan Hennah, Production Designer

Everything about the design of the Kings' tomb was intended to make one feel uncomfortable. It's a very sinister place. The entry shaft slopes down at such a dangerous angle and the walls are sheer. There's a pathway around the side of the chasm, but instead of being cut into the rock it's made up of jutting stones that are crumbling away to make it even more dangerous. When Gandalf is climbing around in there it's the last place you'd want to be, and then the crypts themselves are torn open from the inside.

Alan Lee, Concept Art Director

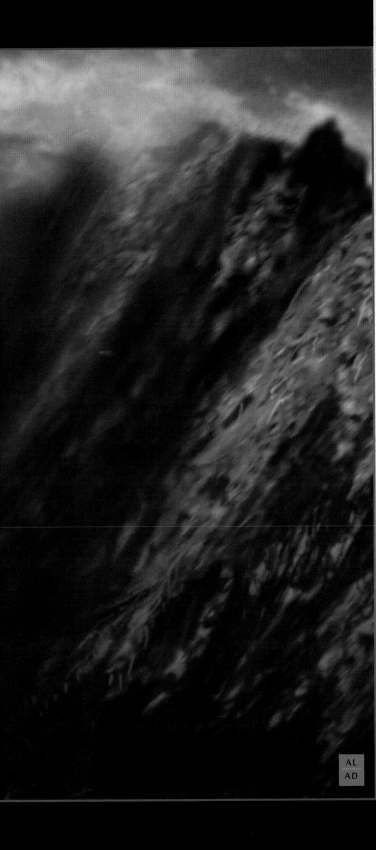

MISTY MOUNTAIN PASS

In the earliest drawings I created for the Misty Mountain Pass I made the rocks around the Dwarves start to resemble faces, as a kind of lead-in to the ideas that the mountains were animate. I didn't think they would do anything at this point, but we would notice as the Company passed them by.

We talked a lot about what these things were and how they might look, and I produced a number of drawings that were like storyboards, exploring possible action in which the rocks came to life and would interact, picking up huge stones to hurl at one another, narrowly missing the Company.

Alan Lee, Concept Art Director

STONE GIANTS

One of the questions on our minds throughout the time we were drawing Stone Giants was, what are these guys made of? Are they creatures whose skin has become so much like rock just from being part of the mountains, sleeping for hundreds of years, something in between rock and flesh but still creatures with muscles and bones, or are they really rock come to life?

I think they are pretty much rock. When bits fall off them as they are hurling boulders around and smashing pieces of each other's heads we don't see exposed bits of insides. It's all rock and dust.

Alan Lee, Concept Art Director

AL
AD

AL
AD

AL
AD

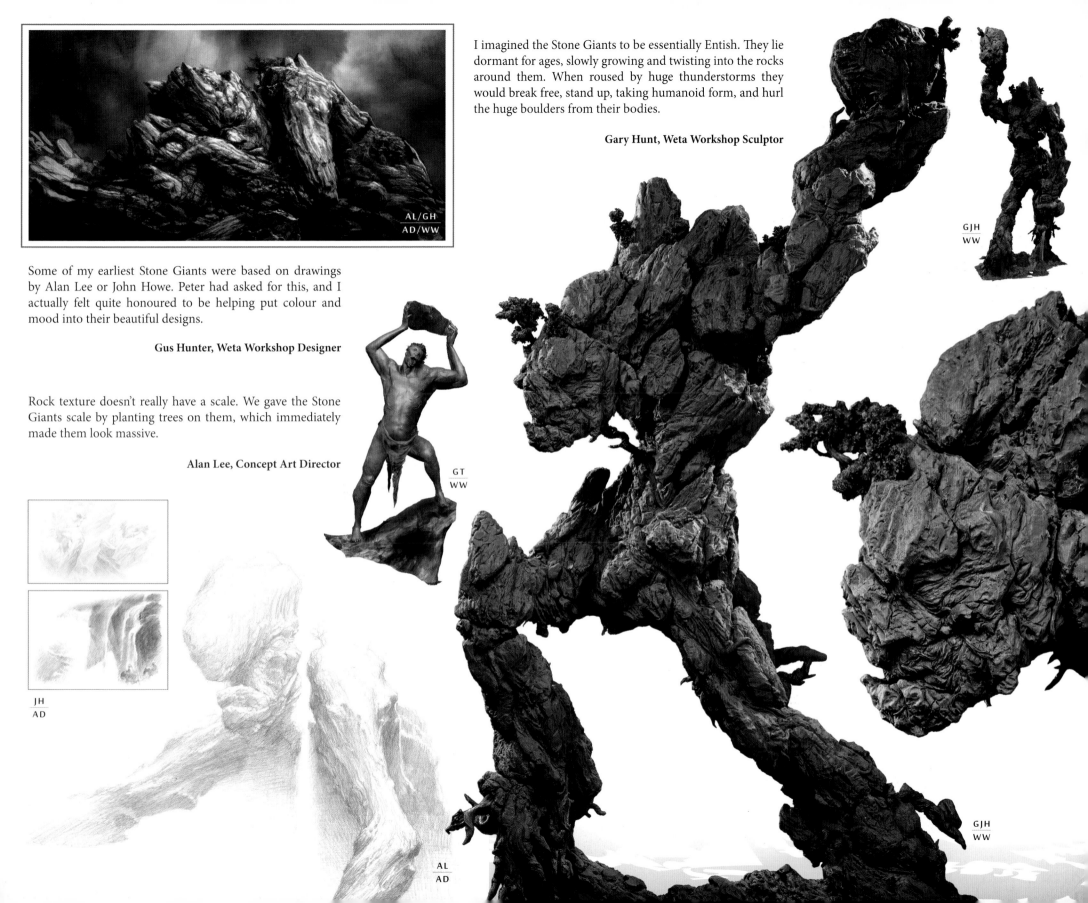

I imagined the Stone Giants to be essentially Entish. They lie dormant for ages, slowly growing and twisting into the rocks around them. When roused by huge thunderstorms they would break free, stand up, taking humanoid form, and hurl the huge boulders from their bodies.

Gary Hunt, Weta Workshop Sculptor

Some of my earliest Stone Giants were based on drawings by Alan Lee or John Howe. Peter had asked for this, and I actually felt quite honoured to be helping put colour and mood into their beautiful designs.

Gus Hunter, Weta Workshop Designer

Rock texture doesn't really have a scale. We gave the Stone Giants scale by planting trees on them, which immediately made them look massive.

Alan Lee, Concept Art Director

GJH
WW

GT
WW

JH
AD

AL
AD

GJH
WW

GH
WW

The Stone Giants were a really interesting project. I personally loved the idea of the Giants being made only of rock that was ripped from the mountain by magical forces. As they moved, the rocks would cascade off their bodies, slowly diminishing their size and requiring them to once again fall back against the mountain to re-merge with the rock, only to rip away from the cliff face reformed again years later.

**Richard Taylor,
Weta Workshop Design & Special Effects Supervisor**

GH
WW

AL
AD

Upon first look in the Misty Mountains you may not see a Stone Giant. Lying in wait, their form is hidden in the structure of the mountain. In the design of the Stone Giants, we wanted to convey this camouflaged nature. Our computer generated Giants are constructed to blend with the rock formations, vegetation, and dressing to the mountains they inhabit. As they reveal themselves and pitch into battle, their size and strength is helped realized through animation and effects. Each movement creates fracturing and detritus obstacles for our heroes.

R. Christopher White, Weta Digital Visual Effects Supervisor

... And Under Hill

DOWN, DOWN TO GOBLIN-TOWN

Taking desperate shelter in a suspiciously hospitable cave, the Dwarves and Bilbo soon fall prey to the Goblins who call the mountains home. Captured and bound, they are marched deep into the cavernous heart of the Misty Mountains and through the nausea-inducing chaos of Goblin-town, a haphazard assemblage of ephemera and horrors passing for a society where the despotic Great Goblin rules as highwayman baron and crown-toting mob boss over a cringing mass of diseased and malformed subjects.

Herein a myriad of gloriously hideous design opportunities would be found with every artist keen to outperform his or her colleagues in conceiving ever more uncomfortable manifestations of the Goblins' debauched and oddly pitiable existence.

The environment itself would be unnerving in the extreme, with its precarious slant and threatening stone maws. The inhabitants of Goblin-town, the leering Goblins, riddled with disfiguring afflictions

and injuries either self or monarch-inflicted, offered the chance to channel private nightmares into reality. Goblin-town is not a pleasant place and it is only too clear that the Dwarves are destined for a grisly fate here unless an intervention can be engineered, especially once Thorin's sword Orcrist is recognized as the Goblin-cleaver, a blade of particular infamy among Middle-earth's dark-lovers.

Overseen by Production Designer Dan Hennah, Goblin-town was built as a studio set, but again, being envisioned at a scale no soundstage could support, would be combined with fully digital environments in the finished film. The Goblins themselves would fluctuate back and forth during the course of their development between being entirely digital or employing some creature suit elements worn by human performers, each technology having significant and differing implications for the Goblin creature design process going on at Weta Workshop.

JH
AD

GOBLIN-TOWN

GOBLIN CAVE TRAP

The Company takes shelter in what looks like quite a hospitable little cave. There is really only one place that is comfortable, so they settle there in this sandy, flat area, and of course it's a trap. Enlightened travellers might have recognized this but Bilbo and the Dwarves lie down, not knowing they're on a trap door until it's too late and they find themselves falling down through a series of holes into a big cage. This is our introduction to Goblin-town, a rambling, haphazard shanty town built into a massive fissure running through the heart of the mountains.

Dan Hennah, Production Designer

A traditional cage is not a terribly exciting structure – bars, door, the whole anchored firmly to the ground … so the cage into which the Dwarves tumble, after a terrifying slide down a crevice, is like a giant taloned fist extended out over the void. They hardly have time to admire the clever design, though, as they are set upon by Goblins and trundled off down into the bowels of the mountains, a place unimaginably worse.

John Howe, Concept Art Director

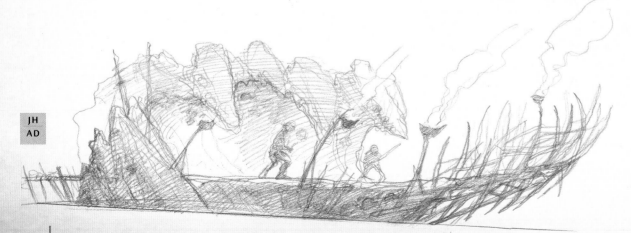

JH
AD

AL
AD

JH
AD

GOBLIN-TOWN ENVIRONMENT

The rock of Goblin-town has its own character. We wanted to get a striated element into the rocks for a lot of drama. There are diagonal cliffs that are very unsettling and dangerous, but then there is also the added element of the erosion. The rock is being eaten away by the various foul juices that have been secreted or oozed by the Goblins and their activities, leaving these holes. It's as rotten an environment as possible.

Alan Lee, Concept Art Director

Goblin-town is all about strong diagonal lines, rickety walkways and fumes and acids rotting the rock and turning it this yucky yellow. We called it hokey pokey!

Dan Hennah, Production Designer

AL
AD

Thinking about the design for the Goblin pathways really started with thinking about the manner of the Dwarves' escape. It was driven by the kind of action that would take place at that part of the story, so we have very flimsy structures on the edge of collapse with a bridge hanging out over the chasm. The way the structures are built into the slanted canyon and stacked as they are makes for a dramatic and terrifying collapse, accumulating as they go down, with buildings sheared off the side of the rock, descending

ATA
WW

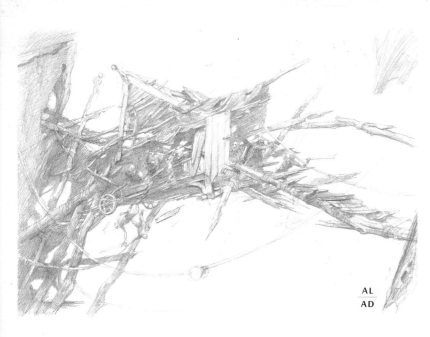

Nothing is more cinematically dull than a big dark hole in the ground, so we went looking for something frightening and uncomfortable. We ended up in a world suspended on platforms. Everything is askew, with jury-rigged platforms hanging over precipices, rickety and precarious. Never mind the Goblins, the very environment is perilous. One misstep and you plummet into goodness knows what, far far below.

John Howe, Concept Art Director

Everything the Goblins have is scavenged and stolen. They are like bottom-end gang members who sit around obsessing over their little triumphs: 'Did you see when he squealed!' They'd gloat and boast over their captives and carry on.

Dan Hennah, Production Designer

AL
——
AD

AL
——
AD

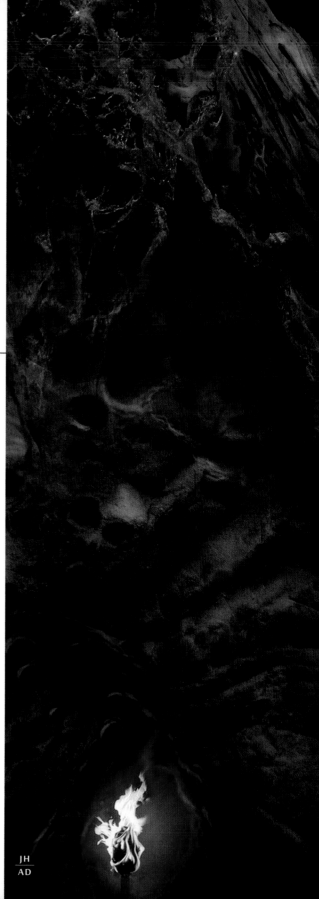

JH
——
AD

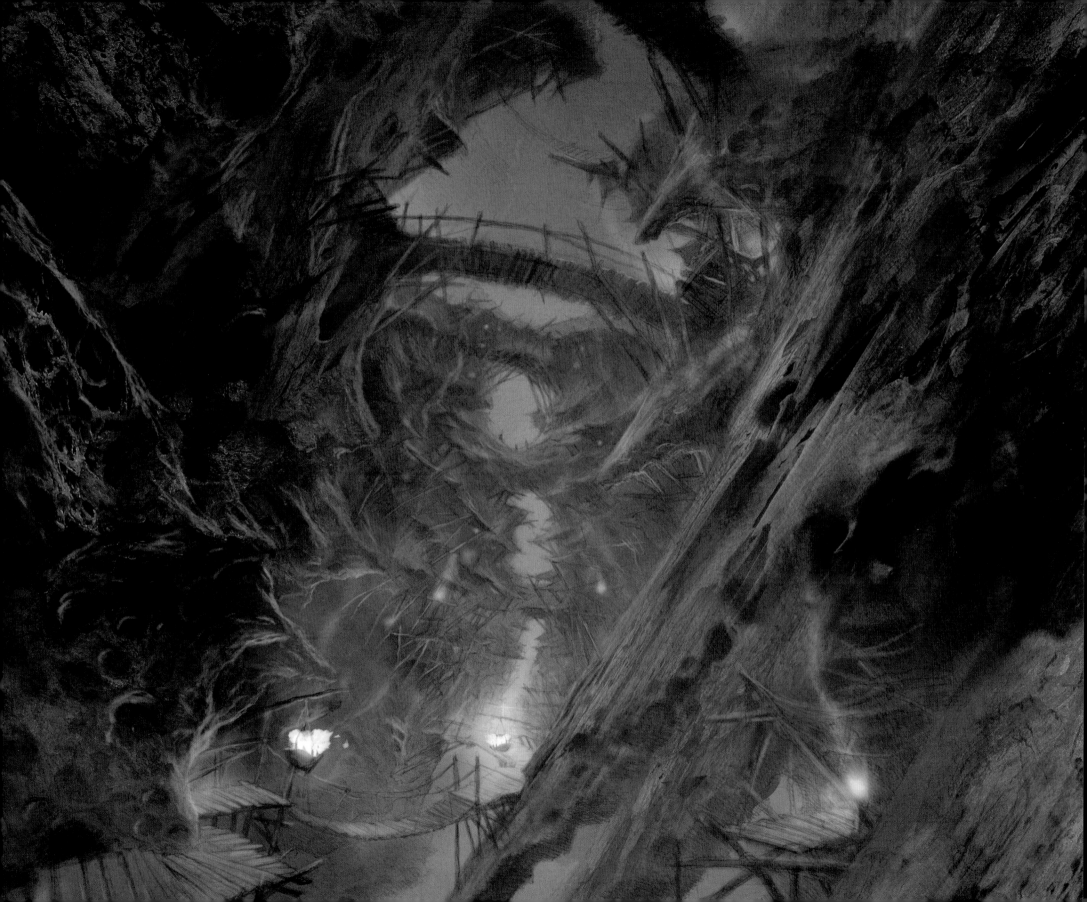

GOBLIN-TOWN DRESSING

The Goblins rob travellers or raid farms and dwellings near the mountains. They either eat or dispose of their captives and sort through their stuff, utilizing what they can in their buildings. Carts, pieces of furniture or buildings, they drag it all back down into their holes in a pathetic attempt to make things homely amongst all the gore.

Alan Lee, Concept Art Director

During the design phase I thought of the Goblins as lice living in a trouser seam.

Dan Hennah, Production Designer

Despite all the chaos and rubbish, the Goblins have a sense of what they find beautiful and arrange objects into totems and effigies. We wanted to give a sense of a variety of Goblin groups, and created horrid heraldic devices to serve as emblems for different clans.

John Howe, Concept Art Director

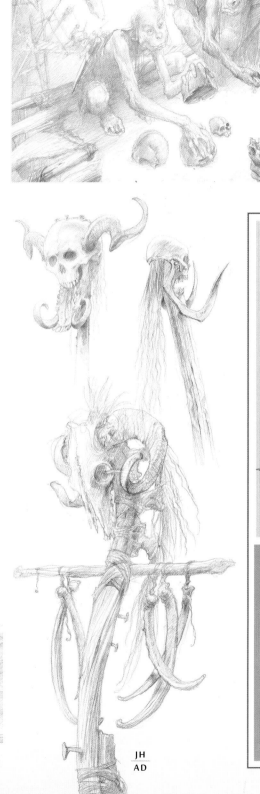

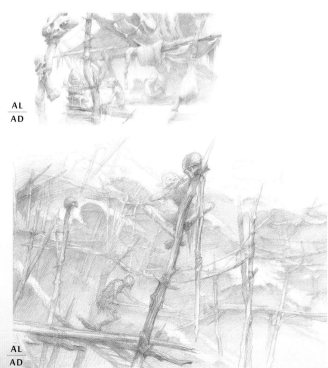

THE GREAT GOBLIN'S THRONE ROOM

The Goblins are plagued by bats, so they have constructed hideous, totem-like, spring-loaded traps all over their town to deal with the problem.

Alan Lee, Concept Art Director

The Great Goblin is this huge, vile creature, but he has some pretensions to being a bit more civilized. He has accumulated things around him that are attempts at showing his refinement. He came upon a king-sized bed at some point which was being transported somewhere. You can almost imagine the moment he saw it and his delight. It's very baroque, covered in cherubs, very gilt and beautiful, and he has turned it into his throne, strung together with rusty straps of iron. It also serves as a commode, with a convenience hole. The set finishers had some fun with this, decorating it with traces of past movements and episodes and with a big bucket underneath, filled with unmentionable horrors.

It had been my idea to have a footstool as well which was made up of compliant Goblins lying on top of one another to allow him to ascend and descend his throne with grace, crunching bones along the way.

Alan Lee, Concept Art Director

AL
AD

THE GREAT GOBLIN

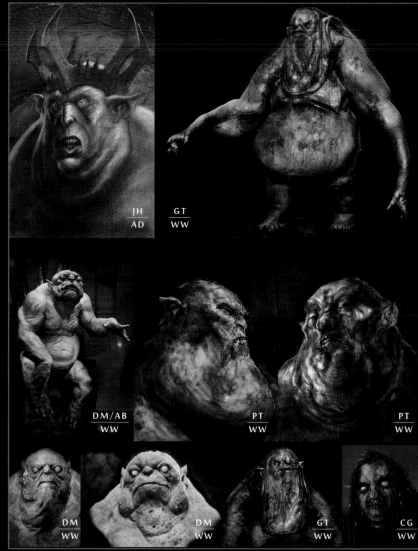

The brief for the Great Goblin was always that of a huge, repulsive, corpulent evil creature. Despite this, in the illustrations and maquettes that I did of the character, I tried to instill a measured degree of charisma and animal magnetism. I thought of him as something between a Dickensian sweatshop operator and a boozed-out rock star who has gone to pot.

David Meng, Weta Workshop Designer

Our design lead for the Great Goblin came by combining the worst qualities of several of Peter's favourites (*left*).

Andrew Baker, Weta Workshop Designer

JB
WW

DM
WW

GH
WW

AJB
WW

AJB
WW

AJB
WW

MR

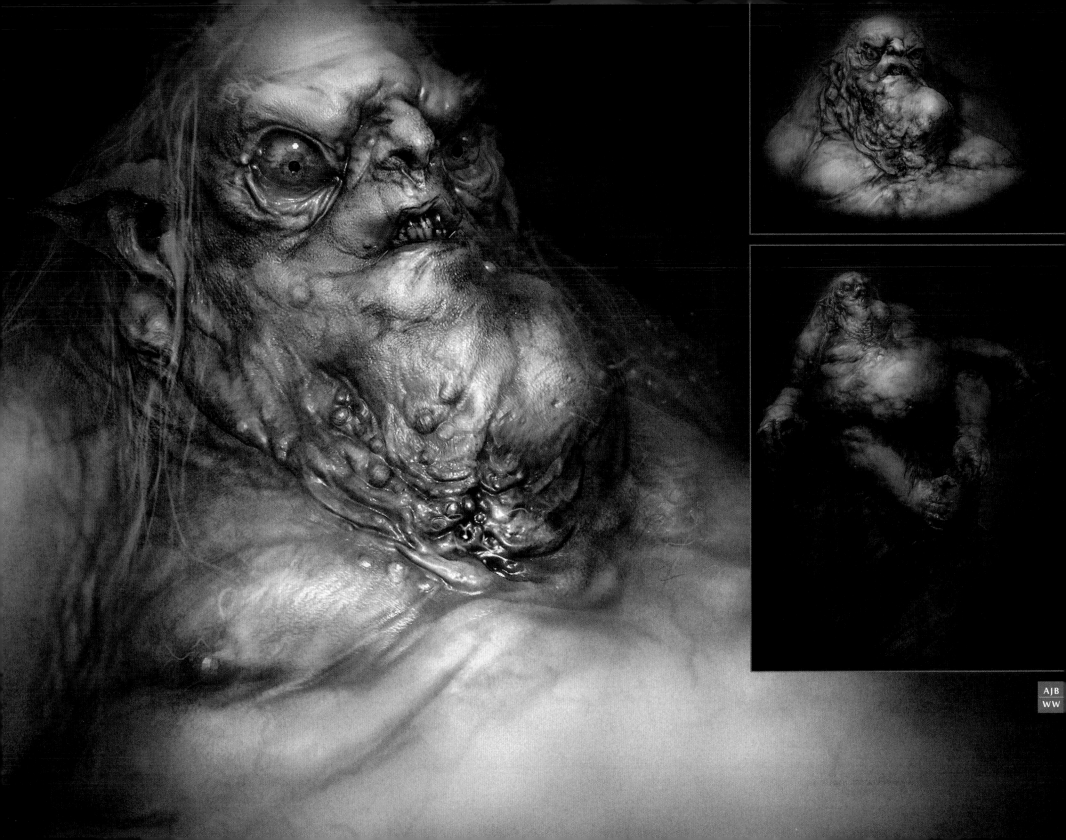

Peter loved the hulking body we had come up with, but as it developed he had us redistribute the Great Goblin's weight to preserve his mobility *(above)*. He ended up with powerful shoulders and a grossly overgrown beer belly as opposed to looking more like a character that couldn't get out of bed *(opposite)*. This kept him looking dangerous and strong.

Once Barry Humphries had been cast to provide the voice, my final design pass was to incorporate a little of Barry into the Great Goblin's face. I played with some expression studies as well, based on Barry's own *(right)*.

Andrew Baker, Weta Workshop Designer

There were severed heads dangling in a bunch from the Great Goblin's sceptre that I had initially thought could be trophies from past conquests. But that's something we've seen so many times before, so I gravitated towards the notion that instead these were all his ex-wives!

Andrew Baker, Weta Workshop Designer

AJB
WW

GOBLINS

EARLY GOBLIN CONCEPTS

The Goblin hordes live deep in the Misty Mountains. They set traps to snare weary travellers attempting to cross the pass. Twisted and deformed, each one is unique. This cast of hundreds had to be created digitally to convey all the nuances needed for the featured goblins and the variations required for our crowds. Translucent tumorous skin and patchy hair are the dominant characteristics of these underground dwellers. Simulated muscles flex and pull as they swipe, scratch and grab at their captives. Their crude weapons, clothes and dwellings are scavenged from the local inhabitants, giving them a rich and varied patchwork quality.

R. Christopher White, Weta Digital Visual Effects Supervisor

Our earliest Goblin designs represented an extrapolation of the Orcs that we'd seen in the earlier films, but with the notion of them being achieved with CGI so they wouldn't have to follow the human form like our old Orcs did. They would be wiry and bow-legged. I remember Tolkien describing Orcs as being reminiscent of the apes of the south, bandy-legged, long-armed, black and hairy.

Jamie Beswarick, Weta Workshop Designer

The earliest concept for the Goblin that became our Scribe was plucked from the generic Goblins by Peter *(above)*. 'If we were going to have a scribe,' he said, 'this guy is going to be him.' Even though we'd revisit and update him as the overall design of the rest of the Goblins evolved, this concept really did set the look for him with his wide-spaced, pug-like eyes.

Andrew Baker, Weta Workshop Designer

We tried all kinds of stuff in the early days of the Goblin designs. Peter threw out a whole pile of potential directions for us to explore, including trying some with piranha-like teeth, some that looked almost undead, some with tiny, mouse-eyes or reptilian faces stretched over a human, some with doglike features, salamander or newt-like concepts, unborn things – all kinds of ideas as we tried to find a strong and original new lead.

The beady, grey, black-eyed concept was the first that Peter really liked *(left)*, but the lead would change and evolve again as we developed it, becoming more bat-like *(above)*.

Andrew Baker, Weta Workshop Designer

Using the 3D sculpting program ZBrush for the Goblins, I was able to create a wide variety of different character looks, pretty much all off the same base model. It's a fast and effective tool for visualising all of my creature and character work. I'll conceptualize in 3D and then paint over them in Photoshop to present to the director.

Andrew Baker, Weta Workshop Designer

… AND UNDER HILL – GOBLINS

GRINNAH

As we were designing and refining the look of the Goblins as a whole, every now and again Peter would zero in on a specific concept and say, 'This guy is going to be a featured character. This guy is the Scribe,' or 'this is Grinnah', for example. Peter had plucked a particular face that he liked for the character of Grinnah and I consequently designed a body to go with it *(right)*, but when he later settled on a newer design as the final Grinnah *(above and far right)*, the previous body ended up becoming the basic generic Goblin body instead.

Grinnah's design is really all about nastiness. He's tight lipped and cruel looking, but as far as Goblins go, probably quite handsome. He represents the ideal in Goblin physique. If you were born a Goblin imp living beneath the Misty Mountains this is the guy you'd aspire to be.

Andrew Baker, Weta Workshop Designer

AJB
WW

THE SCRIBE

Peter had picked out this one Goblin that he liked the look of to be the Great Goblin's royal scribe *(below)*, but he wanted to see him with tiny shrivelled legs *(left)*. The resulting design is my favourite and I was so glad Peter liked him. I invented this story in my head that perhaps he was the Great Goblin's son from some marriage he'd prefer to forget, so he gave him an administration job away from the throne. It's the kind of thing that runs through your mind when you're preoccupied with Goblins for weeks and weeks.

Andrew Baker, Weta Workshop Designer

AJB
WW

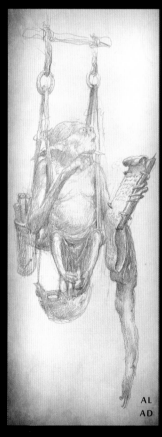

AL
AD

AL
AD

AJB
WW

AJB
WW

AJB
WW

FINAL PHASE GOBLIN CONCEPTS

The Goblins started out as creatures that were to be accomplished entirely digitally, so their designs didn't conform to human performers' proportions, but towards the end of Weta Workshop's involvement in their evolution the plan changed and we began adapting and designing Goblin bodies to be achieved practically as creature suits. That meant humans had to fit inside them, changing their designs and limiting what we could do with their proportions. At that point it was our understanding that we might still have certain hero Goblins that would be digital, but the masses were going to be suits. Peter wanted to see disfiguring lumps and pustules incorporated into these shambling masses, which prompted a huge new round of design and the creation of a large number of suits. In the end, they went back to being entirely digital, but their design carries the legacy of having been intended for physical construction.

Andrew Baker, Weta Workshop Designer

Having the ability to create the Goblins as CG creatures gave us the freedom to pursue some of the more gritty details we saw in the initial concept drawings. We could focus on the dirt, sweat and slime and really enhance the fantastical nature of these characters. Even the most repulsive characters need to have personality and characteristics that help the audience remember and relate to them.

R. Christopher White, Weta Digital Visual Effects Supervisor

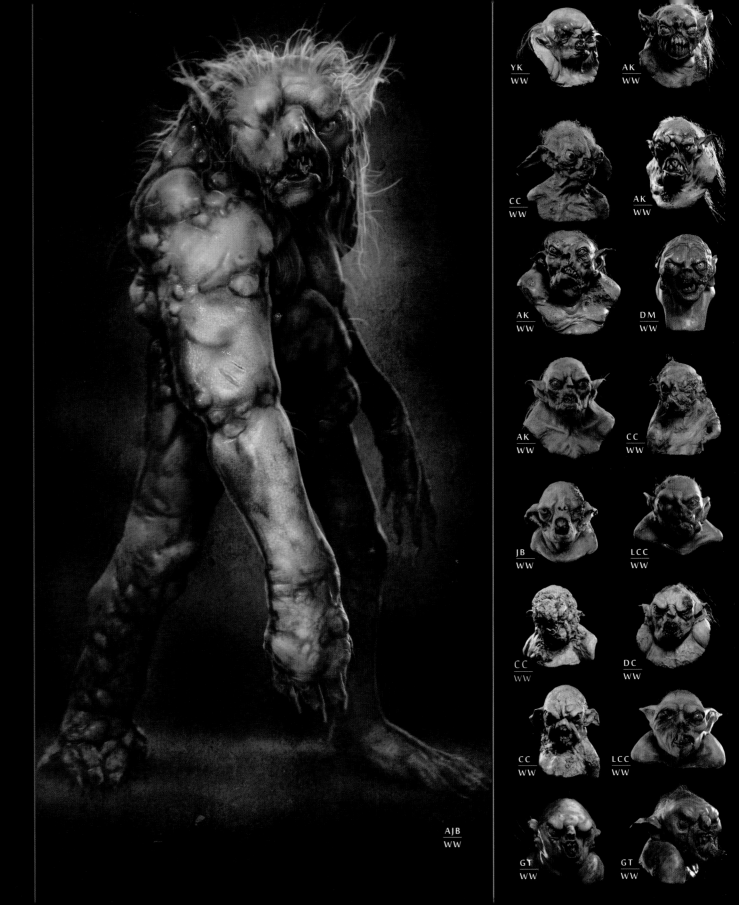

AJB
WW

Riddles in the Dark

'WHAT HAS IT GOT IN ITS POCKETSES?'

Far beneath Goblin-town, in a dark and slimy, seldom visited fissure in the bone of the mountains, Bilbo has his own problems. Being lost is but the start, for on a small island in the middle of a black lake lives Gollum, who is intrigued by his unexpected and decidedly tasty looking visitor.

Gollum's cave was seen briefly in *The Lord of the Rings*, but its geography was not explicitly defined, affording the Art Department Conceptual Artists and Production Designer plenty of scope to come up with a memorable look for this unpleasant and forgotten corner of Middle-earth. They would exploit its inhospitability for poor lost, frightened Bilbo to maximum effect and set up the danger which only his wits and a little good luck will eventually see him escape.

Returning to embody the deliciously watchable Gollum once again was Andy Serkis, who played the character in the trilogy. This time round Andy would also take on the responsibility of Second Unit Director, adding it to his collection of roles to play on the project along side Gollum's own multiple personalities. Since *The Lord of the Rings* Andy had forged a close working relationship with Peter Jackson, having had roles in both Peter's *King Kong* and *The Adventures of Tintin*, and starring as Caesar in *Rise of the Planet of the Apes*, which Weta Digital worked on, transforming him into the film's digital ape leader.

IMAGE (LEFT) COURTESY OF WARNER BROS. PICTURES

Gollum's Cave

Descending into Gollum's realm, we enter an area where the rocks are very much a continuation of what we've seen above in Goblin-town, with the diagonal fissuring and the pitted, rotten look like yellow hokey-pokey cavities in great big jagged teeth. Even the lake has an acidic value to it. It's not clean, clear water. This visual link reinforces that these two environments are geographically linked. Bilbo is down here and in trouble, just as the Dwarves are, up above.

Lighting in caves is always something of a cinematic cheat. In this instance we can say that the geographic anomaly that has created this fault opens all the way up to the sky, far above. There are chasms through which shafts of sunlight or moonlight beam down, but more often these are via a double bounce, so it's a dim ambience like being in the bottom of a big sink hole. Goblin-town also had its torches, which gave it a warmer light, but down in Gollum's Cave it's filtered moonlight bouncing off the water.

Dan Hennah, Production Designer

JH
AD

My paintings of Gollum's Cave began with bringing colour to some of Alan Lee and John Howe's pencil concepts, but Peter also told me to go off on my own tangent and come up with some of my own ideas as well, which is a great thing to be told. Most of the environment studies I produced were a combination of both, with Alan and John's influence, but some of my stuff as well.

Gus Hunter, Weta Workshop Designer

Gollum's cave environment adheres closely to what is described in the book, a little island set in a wide underground lake with a sloping shore.

Alan Lee, Concept Art Director

GH
WW

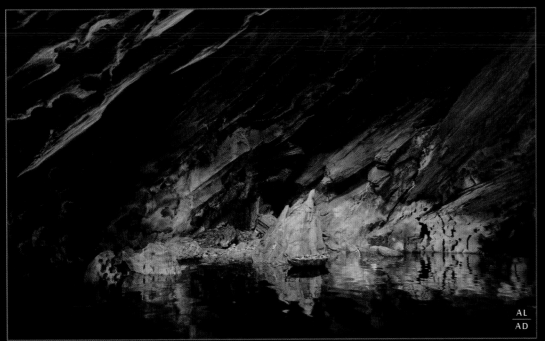

The colour palette for the rocks of Gollum's Cave consisted of blue under-painting with red oxides and what we called hokey-pokey – these acid-eaten, yellow ochre, pitted areas that look noxious and decayed. It was an interesting colour that provided contrast with the darker rock of the cave walls and Goblin-town.

There were also mushrooms. Bilbo falls down into them and ends up with some in his mouth. We started out painting them a certain way, but had to bump the colour up to make them look more visible and poisonous.

Kathryn Lim, Set Finishing Supervisor

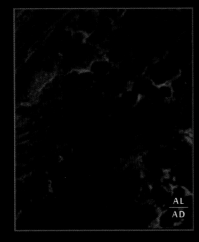

GOLLUM

GOLLUM'S CORACLE

When we come upon Gollum in *The Hobbit*, we find a slimy, aggressive creature who mutters monologues, referring to himself in the third person. Visually you could almost say that he looks like a large malnourished toad possessing vicious strength coupled with two conflicting personalities. He has giant blue retro-reflective eyes. His teeth are few and are worn down, full of chips and cracks. His skin is very pale and translucent, with dirt found around his feet, hands and knees. His hair is shoulder length, very thin with a bit of curl. He wears nothing but a simple loin cloth.

Jeff Capogreco, Weta Digital Effects Supervisor

The Hobbit is filled with scenes that take place in the dark. It was a wacky notion, but trying to reconcile the lack of light and the book's description of Gollum as having glowing green eyes, I thought perhaps the cave might be infested with luminous invertebrates that cast an eerie green light over everything, reflecting in the lake and Gollum's sensitive eyes? Perhaps he'd eat them too, giving him a mouthful of glowing teeth and saliva?

Daniel Falconer, Weta Workshop Designer

Gollum's coracle is made of bits of Goblin skin, bones and a few twigs. He has very limited materials down there so he's made quite a serviceable little vessel with what he had at hand. It's unclear in the book exactly what his boat was made of or how it got there, but this felt to us like a good, practical alternative to something more traditional.

Alan Lee, Concept Art Director

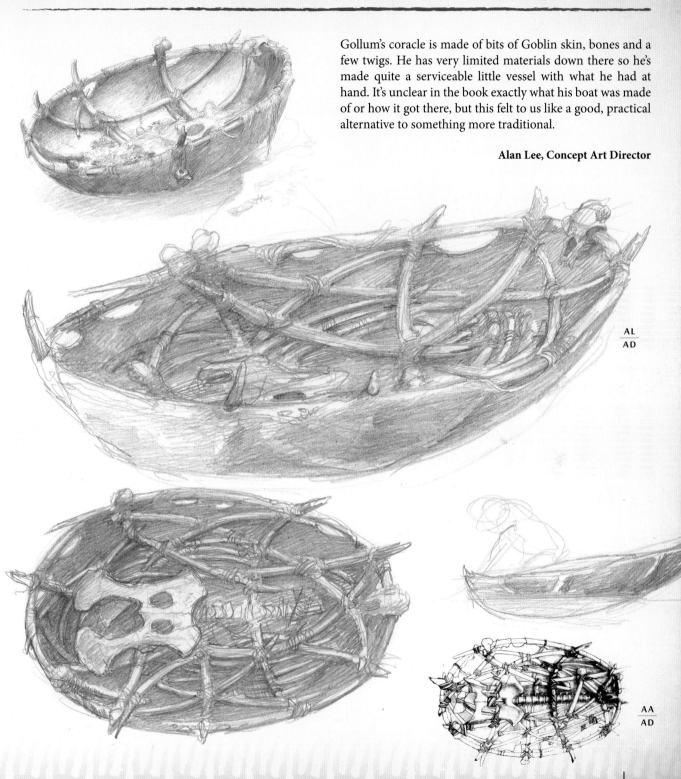

Out of the Frying Pan into the Fire

'ESCAPING GOBLINS TO BE CAUGHT BY WOLVES!'

Reunited, but fleeing pursuit, the Dwarves, hobbit and wizard take to the trees to remain out of reach of vengeful Warg-riders. Gandalf's use of fire to deter their pursuers earns them short-lived satisfaction, but becomes its own peril, for the hillside is dry and vulnerable to the flames. Were it not for the Eagles, this might have been the end of their quest.

Reappearing in revised forms are the rapacious Wargs, watchers of *The Lord of the Rings* will remember, complete with malicious riders. This time, however, the variety encountered are a northerly breed with more wolf-like features, so they offered a new design opportunity for the creature specialists charged with designing them. Peter Jackson was also keen to see something distinctive in their riders' costuming.

The environment in which the conflagration would occur also require careful consideration and, due to the nature of the action, would have to be designed and built as a studio set so that all aspects of the scene could be controlled, and be rebuilt more than once.

JH
AD

WARG ATTACK

The trees the Dwarves climb are these old mountain pines, very old but not huge. They're dry and rotten around the bases so the idea is that while Wargs can't climb trees, they can certainly dig the roots away and try to push them over, forcing the Dwarves further out towards the edge of the drop-off where Gandalf is perched. And then there's the fire. It's all about building jeopardy and stacking layers of peril so the threat to our heroes keeps ratcheting up all the way through the scene.

Dan Hennah, Production Designer

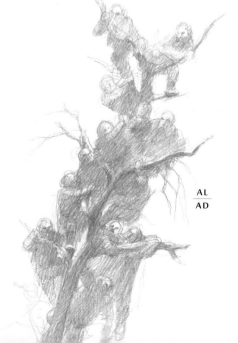

WARGS

I tried to keep some wolf form in my Wargs. They're basically meant to be demon-wolves so I tried to give them an almost demonic emaciated, vicious look.

Paul Tobin, Weta Workshop Designer

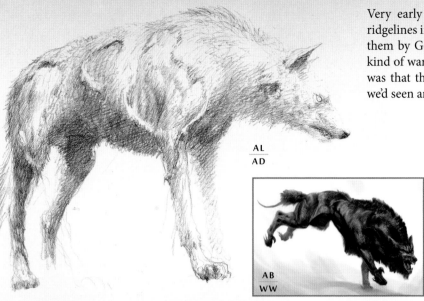

Very early in the design process we played with putting ridgelines into the fur of the Wargs. Maybe it was shaved into them by Goblins or perhaps it was biological, maybe some kind of war marking they do, or something else. What stuck was that these Wargs would be more wolf-like than others we'd seen and there was the idea of a white furred matriarch.

Nick Keller, Weta Workshop Designer

The Wargs we meet in the Misty Mountains are quite different than those we saw in *The Two Towers*; we are further north in *The Hobbit*, and the Wargs are akin to timber wolves: nightmare silhouettes, far larger and vastly more ferocious.

John Howe, Concept Art Director

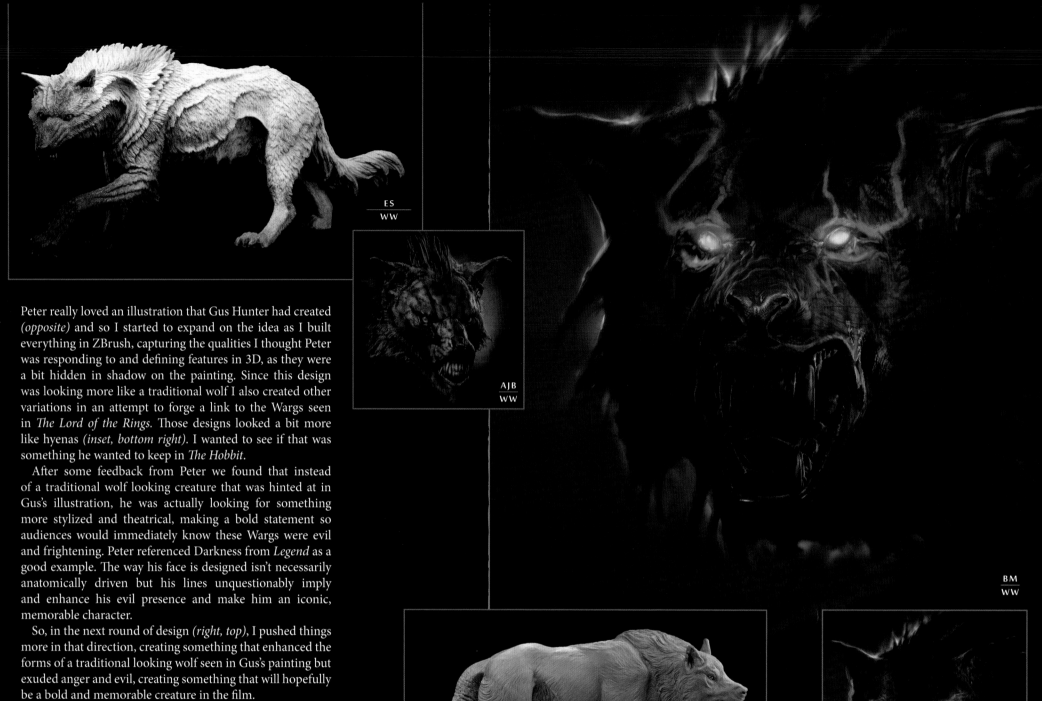

ES
WW

AJB
WW

BM
WW

Peter really loved an illustration that Gus Hunter had created *(opposite)* and so I started to expand on the idea as I built everything in ZBrush, capturing the qualities I thought Peter was responding to and defining features in 3D, as they were a bit hidden in shadow on the painting. Since this design was looking more like a traditional wolf I also created other variations in an attempt to forge a link to the Wargs seen in *The Lord of the Rings.* Those designs looked a bit more like hyenas *(inset, bottom right).* I wanted to see if that was something he wanted to keep in *The Hobbit.*

After some feedback from Peter we found that instead of a traditional wolf looking creature that was hinted at in Gus's illustration, he was actually looking for something more stylized and theatrical, making a bold statement so audiences would immediately know these Wargs were evil and frightening. Peter referenced Darkness from *Legend* as a good example. The way his face is designed isn't necessarily anatomically driven but his lines unquestionably imply and enhance his evil presence and make him an iconic, memorable character.

So, in the next round of design *(right, top),* I pushed things more in that direction, creating something that enhanced the forms of a traditional looking wolf seen in Gus's painting but exuded anger and evil, creating something that will hopefully be a bold and memorable creature in the film.

Ben Mauro, Weta Workshop Designer

JB
WW

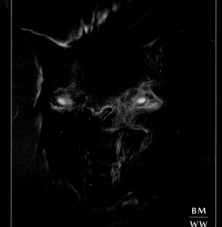

BM
WW

WARG RIDERS

The Warg-riding Orcs needed a new look. We played with graphic motifs using black and white. Maybe the Orcs were using disgusting, poorly cured hides and leathers and working with bones or tusks to create forms they thought would be intimidating. There are a lot of big forward-facing spikes in some of these designs, which look dangerous and probably aren't very practical, but we were pursuing an aesthetic.

I also looked for new kinds of weapons they could use while mounted, though perhaps some of these ideas went a bit too far out there. It was worth trying for the fun of it.

Nick Keller, Weta Workshop Designer

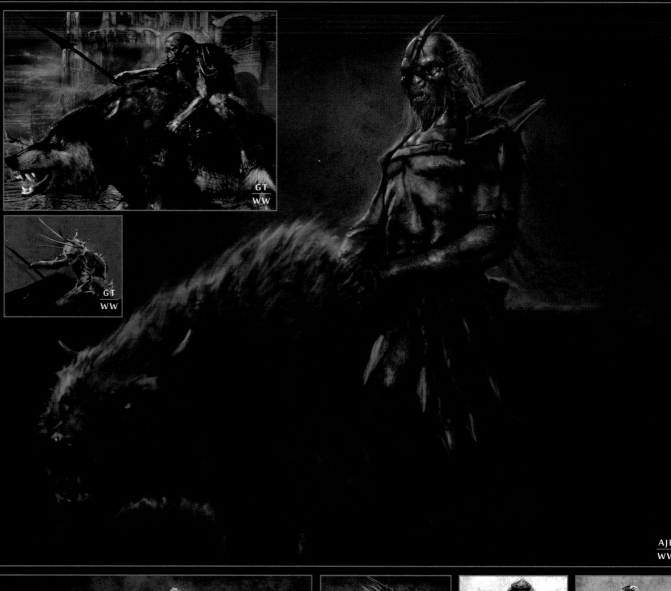

GT
WW

GT
WW

AJB
WW

SL
WW

AJB
WW

AJB
WW

DF
WW

DF
WW

NK
WW

NK
WW

NK/DF
WW

NK
WW

DF
WW

NK
WW

NK
WW

NK
WW

THE CARROCK

The Eagles rescue the Dwarves, Gandalf and Bilbo, dropping them off at the Carrock, which marks the edge of Beorn's lands. We thought it might be interesting if, from a certain angle this bald, jutting rock might be evocative of a bear, into which Beorn has cut a winding stairway.

Alan Lee, Concept Art Director

JH
AD

AL
AD

AL
AD

AL
AD

As a final environment for *The Hobbit: An Unexpected Journey* the Carrock is an ideal choice for the Art Department. It hints at where we are in Middle-earth and where we might be going when we come back. From this elevated position one can see the eastern Misty Mountains, the Anduin Valley and right across the vast Mirkwood Forest to catch light shining on the distant Lonely Mountain. Beorn has hewn stairs into the living rock so he can come here to contemplate his world.

It is a natural rock formation that, to Beorn, resembles a bear, possibly his father. For us it was a fine line between finding an image of a bear in nature and avoiding having it look like a man-made sculpture. After extensive concept work and modelling, our artists, modellers, chippies, sculptors, painters, Greens team and dressers have all collaborated to create a stunning set for Peter to film his last scene of the film on.

Dan Hennah, Production Designer

About the Peninsula

ART DEPARTMENT

The 3 Foot 7 Art Department, led by Production Designer Dan Hennah, is responsible for creating the overall look of the film, bringing the Director's vision to the screen. The Art Department is responsible for creating all of the sets, props and dressings from concepts through to the finished articles. Their job is to create an environment that is so real, the actors feel completely in character wherever that may be: in a forest, on a lake, up a tree or in a cave. To achieve a look or atmosphere for a film involves many people. The Art Department on *The Hobbit* has over 350 artists and craftspeople in workshops throughout the Miramar Peninsula. Starting with the Director's brief, ideas going through the concept stage before being turned into working drawings. Designs then go to the various departments to be made into a physical set, prop or dressing.

COSTUME DEPARTMENT

The Costume Department is ultimately responsible for the look worn by actors, stunt performers and body doubles in front of the camera. The department consists of 'off set' and 'on set' crew, each dealing specifically with either producing the costumes or dressing and maintaining the look and continuity during filming. 'Off set' crew are based in the workroom where designs are created, illustrations coloured, samples developed, materials sourced, patterns cut, fabric dyed, jewellery made, boots cobbled, costumes fitted and alterations completed. Finished costumes are aged to appear lived in. 'On set' crew work either in the studio or travel to location. As well as dressing the performers, they also attend to their comfort and safety by keeping them warm or cool between shots and attend to general maintenance and laundry. Continuity photos are taken and notes are written about how the costumes were worn for that particular scene. On *The Hobbit* the Costume Department consists of approximately 60 'off set' crew and 15 'on set' crew.

MAKE-UP & HAIR DEPARTMENT

The 3 Foot 7 Make-up Department creates characters by designing and applying make-up, prosthetics, wigs and the beards to the cast. Every cast member, including extras, wear some form of wig and all the lead actors and their various doubles wear prosthetics. Four make-up department bases manage the large number of artists and extras. All activity is coordinated through the Make-up Room based at Stone Street Studios. This is also where wigs are made and mended, and hair is prepared for inclusion in the wigs, including the dying and curling. Seven five-seater Make-up Trucks positioned on the back-lot are used for applying prosthetics, make-up and hair on principal actors, some taking three hours to complete each day, under the eye of two supervisors. Offsite is another 18-station make-up facility for extras. There are 34 permanent staff though the department swells to as many as 60 during periods that call for large numbers of extras and stunt people.

WETA WORKSHOP

Weta Workshop is a multi-award winning conceptual design and manufacturing facility based in Wellington, New Zealand, servicing the world's creative industries. Weta Workshop draws on more than 25 years of film-making experience and is led by five-times Academy Award®-winner, Richard Taylor. Their crew members are expert in a diverse range of disciplines and enjoy engaging in projects, from preliminary technical analysis and conceptual design through to manufacture and final delivery of product, anywhere in the world. Weta Workshop provides design and manufacturing services on *The Hobbit*, designing creatures, armour and weapons, and building armour, weapons, prosthetics and physical creature effects.

WETA DIGITAL

Weta Digital is one of the world's premier visual effects companies. Led by Senior Visual Effects Supervisor Joe Letteri, Weta Digital is known for uncompromising creativity and commitment to developing innovative technology. From ground-breaking performance-driven digital characters like Gollum, Kong and Caesar, to the revolutionary virtual production workflows of *Avatar* and *The Adventures of Tintin*, Weta Digital's team continues to break down barriers between live action and computer-generated imagery and expand what is possible in film. Weta Digital established its reputation for cutting edge visual effects with work on blockbusters like *The Lord of the Rings trilogy* and *King Kong*. The company began work in 1993 on co-founder Peter Jackson's film *Heavenly Creatures* and is based in a number of facilities spread around Wellington, New Zealand. Weta Digital is creating all digital visual effects on *The Hobbit* films.

You can also keep up to date on all our new releases as well as all the Weta news, including *The Hobbit: An Unexpected Journey*, by signing up for our free email newsletter at: www.wetaNZ.com

COLLECTIBLE ART

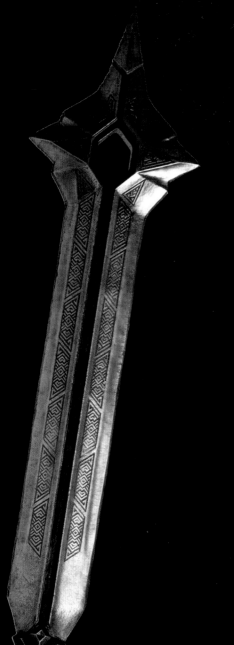

The same burning passion and relentless pursuit of perfection that drives every department bringing Middle-earth to life for *The Hobbit – An Unexpected Journey* also goes into the creation of the most authentic movie replicas. Created by the same artists working on the films, Weta is sourcing beautiful Middle-earth artefacts from across the departments and companies represented in *The Hobbit, An Unexpected Journey*, and offering them as authentic replicas for discerning collectors.

The line represents the closest experience next to visiting into Middle-earth itself. Collectors will find replica swords hand forged by a world renown master swordsmith using centuries old and cutting edge techniques and props cast from the very same moulds as those made for the films. Maps and calligraphic prop replicas have been hand-made and the films' original artists have created new, limited edition art prints based on the characters and landscapes they helped imagine for the films.

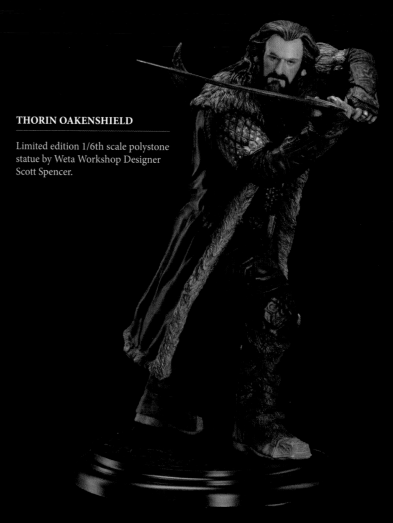

THORIN OAKENSHIELD

Limited edition 1/6th scale polystone statue by Weta Workshop Designer Scott Spencer.

THORIN'S EREBOR KEY

Accurate prop replica cast from moulds taken directly from the 3 Foot 7 Art Department. Thorin's Erebor Key prop, was designed by Concept Art Director John Howe and made by the production's Art Department.

BALIN'S MACE

Accurate prop replica cast from the same molds as Balin's Mace prop, made by Weta Workshop Master Swordsmith Peter Lyon and designed by Weta Workshop Designer Frank Victoria.

THORIN'S MAP

Authentically aged prop replica created by 3 Foot 7 Art Department Graphic Artist Daniel Reeve.

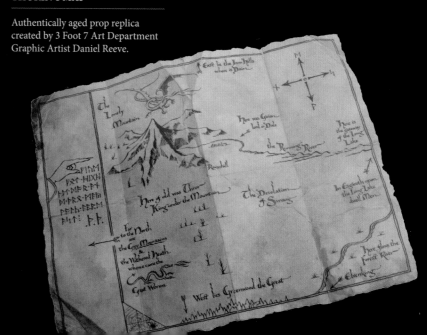

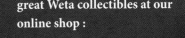

AN UNEXPECTED JOURNEY

Limited edition art print by Weta Workshop
Designer Gus Hunter.

GANDALF THE GREY

Limited edition 1/6th scale polystone statue by
Weta Workshop Sculptor Steven Saunders.

CREDITS

BOOK CREDITS

Writer and Art Director	Daniel Falconer
Layout Artist	Monique Hamon
Art Department Content Co-ordinator	Karen Flett
Image Retouching	Stuart Thomas
Transcribers	Candace Little
	Darinie Johnston
Weta Workshop Design & Special Effects Supervisor	Richard Taylor
Weta Workshop Manager	Tania Rodger
Weta Ltd General Manager	Tim Launder
Weta Publishing Manager	Kate Jorgensen
Weta Workshop Design Studio Manager	Richard Athorne
Weta Workshop Photography	Steve Unwin
	Wendy Brown
	Simon Godsiff

HarperCollins*Publishers* UK

Chris Smith	Series Editor
Charles Light	Production Director
Terence Caven	Design Manager

ABOUT THE AUTHOR

Daniel Falconer has been a designer at Weta Workshop for more than fifteen years, producing conceptual art as part of the design team on many of the company's high profile projects including *The Lord of the Rings*, *King Kong*, *The Chronicles of Narnia*, *Avatar*, and now *The Hobbit*. Daniel has written a number of books for Weta; *The World of Kong*, *The Crafting of Narnia*, *Weta: The Collector's Guide* and *The Art of District 9*, each showcasing the company's creative works.

Daniel lives and works in Wellington, New Zealand with his wife Catherine and two daughters, revelling in his dream career of playing in imaginary worlds every day.

CONTRIBUTOR CREDITS

3 Foot 7 Ltd Art Department (AD)

The 3 Foot 7 Art Department, lead by Production Designer Dan Hennah, is responsible for creating the overall look of the film, which helps to bring the Director's vision to the screen. The Art Department is responsible for creating all of the sets, props & dressings from concepts through to the finished articles.

Dan Hennah	Production Designer	DH
Alan Lee	Concept Art Director	AL
John Howe	Concept Art Director	JH
Nick Weir	Prop Master	
Ra Vincent	Set Decorator	RV
Paul Gray	Prop Making Supervisor	
Kathryn Lim	Set Finishing Supervisor	
Letty Macphedran	Soft Furnishing Designer	LM
Anthony Allan	Prop Designer	AA
Link Choi	Prop Designer	LC
Mat Hunkin	Prop Designer	MH
Matt Smith	Prop Designer	MS
Stephen Templer	Prop Designer	ST

3 Foot 7 Ltd Costume Department (CD)

The Costume Department is ultimately responsible for the look worn by actors, stunt performers and body doubles in front of the camera. The department consists of 'off set' and 'on set' crew, each dealing specifically with either producing the costumes or dressing and maintaining the look and continuity during filming.

Ann Maskrey	Costume Designer	AM
Bob Buck	Additional Costume Designer	BB

3 Foot 7 Ltd Make-up Department

The 3 Foot 7 Make-up Department creates characters by designing and applying make-up, prosthetics, wigs and the beards to the cast. Every cast member, including extras, wear some form of wig and all the lead actors and their various doubles wear prosthetics.

Peter King	Make-up and Hair Designer

Weta Workshop (WW)

Weta Workshop is a multi-award winning conceptual design and manufacturing facility based in Wellington, New Zealand. Best known for its Academy Award® winning work on *The Lord of the Rings* trilogy, Weta Workshop has contributed conceptual design (creatures, characters and environments) for *The Hobbit* films along with manufacturing armour, weapons, specialty prosthetics and creatures. Weta Workshop is led by Academy Award® winner Richard Taylor.

Richard Taylor	Design & Special Effects Supervisor	
Aaron Beck	Weta Workshop Designer	AB
Adam Anderson	Weta Workshop Designer	ATA
Andrew Baker	Weta Workshop Designer	AJB
Avis Kolokontes	Weta Workshop Sculptor	AK
Ben Mauro	Weta Workshop Designer	BM
Chris Guise	Weta Workshop Designer	CG
Craig Campbell	Weta Workshop Sculptor	CC
Daniel Cockersell	Weta Workshop Sculptor	DC
Daniel Falconer	Weta Workshop Designer	DF
David Meng	Weta Workshop Sculptor	DM
Ed Denton	Weta Workshop 3D Model Maker	ED
Eden Small	Weta Workshop Sculptor	ES
Eduardo Pena	Weta Workshop Designer	EP
Frank Victoria	Weta Workshop Designer	FV
Gary Hunt	Weta Workshop Sculptor	GJH
Gus Hunter	Weta Workshop Designer	GH
Greg Tozer	Weta Workshop Designer	GT
Johnny Fraser-Allen	Weta Workshop Designer	JFA
Jamie Beswarick	Weta Workshop Designer	JB
Lindsey Crummett	Weta Workshop Designer	LCC
Matthew Rodgers	Weta Workshop Designer	MR
Nick Keller	Weta Workshop Designer	NK
Paul Tobin	Weta Workshop Designer	PT
Scott Spencer	Weta Workshop Designer	SS
Steve Lambert	Weta Workshop Designer	SL
William Furneaux	Weta Workshop Designer	WF
Yasmin Khudari	Weta Workshop Sculptor	YK

Weta Digital

Weta Digital is one of the world's premier visual effects companies. Led by Senior Visual Effects Supervisor Joe Letteri, Weta Digital is known for uncompromising creativity and commitment to developing innovative technology. Weta Digital established its reputation for cutting edge visual effects with work on blockbusters like *The Lord of the Rings* trilogy and *King Kong*. The company began work in 1993 on co-founder Peter Jackson's film *Heavenly Creatures* and is based in a number of facilities spread around Wellington, New Zealand. Weta Digital is creating all digital visual effects on *The Hobbit* films.

R. Christopher White	Visual Effects Supervisor
Jeff Capogreco	Digital Effects Supervisor

Thanks to: Peter Jackson, Fran Walsh, Philippa Boyens, Zane Weiner, Caro Cunningham, Brigitte Yorke, Matt Dravitzki, Amanda Walker, Rachel Gilkison, Dan Hennah, Chris Hennah, Karen Flett, Natalie Crane, Graeme Carlisle, Judy Alley, Ceris Price, Guy Campbell, Seamus Kavanah, Dave Gouge, Mahria Sangster, Amy Minty, Ri Streeter and Tracey Morgan.

NB.   Film credits were not available at the time of publication.

ARTWORK CREDIT KEY

Artist credit as indicated on top and their department indicated beneath line	AL —— AD
All artwork on page by indicated artist and department	

BILBO'S
BURGLAR CONTRACT

...contained herein [the conditions of Engagement] by signing or making their marks in the spaces provided for so doing, and affixing seals if applicable.

The witnesses to this Contract, being those others whose signatures, marks or seals are affixed hereto affirm, state and declare their understanding and unbiased agreement to all that is contained herein.

CONFIDENTIALITY is of utmost importance and must be strictly maintained at all times. During the course of his employment with the Company, Burglar will hear, see, learn, apprehend, comprehend, and, in short, gain knowledge of particular facts, ideas, plans, strategies, theories, geography, cartography, iconography, means, tactics and/or policies, whether actual, implicit, conceptual, historical or fanciful. Burglar undertakes and agrees to maintain this knowledge in utmost secrecy and confidentiality, and to neither divulge nor make known said knowledge by any means, including but not limited to speech, writing, demonstration, re-enactment, mime, or signage and retrieval within means or apparatus currently known or unknown of as yet unthought of—

EARLY TERMINATION of this Contract shall attract an early termination fee—to be determined by Thorin and Company at their sole and absolute discretion. All clauses contained herein shall survive such termination and remain enforceable—in all countries whether existent now or in the future, throughout the known world.

DISPUTES arising between the Contract Parties shall be heard and judged by an arbitrator of the Company's choosing, and all fees shall be pleaded, delivered, defended, answered, debated and judged in the Dwarvish tongue.

In the event of a dispute arising in relation to the terms of this Agreement, the non-prevailing party shall reimburse the prevailing party for all reasonable fees and costs resulting therefrom.

If any provision of this Contract is held unenforceable, then such provision shall be modified to reflect the Parties' intention. All remaining provisions of this Contract shall remain in full force and effect.

The failure—by one party to require performance of any provision herein shall not affect that party's right to require performance at any time thereafter, nor shall a waiver of any breach or default of this Contract constitute a waiver of any subsequent breach or default of a waiver of the provision itself.

Wherefore—each of the Parties agree that any action in relation to an alleged breach of this Agreement shall be commenced within one year of the date of the breach, without regard to the date the breach is discovered. Any action not brought within that one (1) year time period shall be barred, without regard to any other limitations period set forth herein.

All conditions imposed herein are deemed to survive—loss or destruction of this document, whether by accident or wilful mishap. For means of foul, and any reconstruction, re-working, updating or improvements or additions made shall include a condition similar to this condition, notwithstanding any repetition, reformation, over-statement or implication hereby recognised or disclosed.

Any and all damages brought against the Company by third parties, whether during the course of the Adventure or subsequent to it, shall be borne by the Company and the Burglar on a pro-rata basis, but the reverse situation does not apply.

No recompense for loss of income due to an extended absence shall apply. Burglar is deemed to be "at the service of" Thorin and Company until released therefrom.

Specialist equipment required in the execution of duties in his professional role as Burglar shall be purchased, procured, fashioned or obtained by Burglar, in whatsoever method he may see fit.

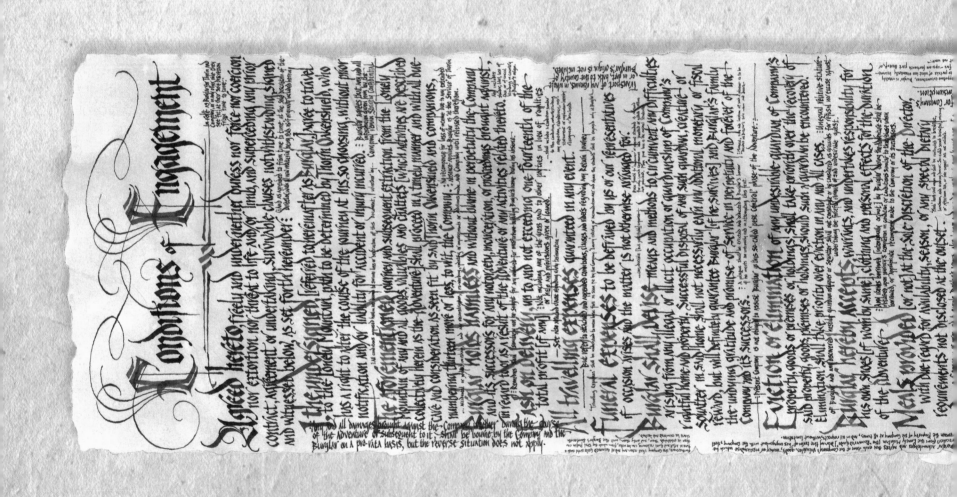

Conditions of Engagement

Agreed hereto, freely and undertaking, duress nor force nor coercion, nor extortion, nor threat to life and/or limb, and superceding any prior contract, agreement or undertaking, survivable clauses notwithstanding, signed and witnessed below, as set forth hereunder:

The undersigned, [referred to hereinafter as Burglar,] agree to travel to the Lonely Mountain, path to be determined by Thorin Oakenshield, who has a right to alter the course of the journey at his so choosing, without prior notification and/or liability for accident or injury incurred.

The aforementioned journey and subsequent extraction from the Lonely Mountain of any and all goods, valuables and chattels [which activities are described collectively herein as the Adventure] shall proceed in a timely manner and with all due care and consideration as seen fit by said Thorin Oakenshield and companions, numbering thirteen more or less, to wit, the Company...

Burglar holds harmless and without blame in perpetuity the Company and its successors for any indirect, inconsequential, or direct damages brought against the Company...

All travelling expenses guaranteed in any event...

Funeral expenses to be defrayed by us or our representatives if occasion arises and the matter is not otherwise resolved for.

Burglar shall avise means and methods to circumvent any difficulties arising from any illegal or illicit occupation or guardianship of Company's rightful home and property. Successful disposal of any such guardian, creature or counter in said home shall not necessarily earn any additional monetary or fiscal reward, but will definitely guarantee Burglar life sacrifices and Burglar's family, the undying gratitude and promise of service in perpetuity and forever of the Company and its successors.

Eviction or elimination of any undesirable guardian of Company's property, goods or premises or holdings shall take precedence over the recovery of said property, goods, premises or holdings, should such a guardian be encountered. Elimination shall take priority over eviction in any and all cases.

Burglar hereby accepts warranties, and undertakes responsibility for his own shoes [if worn by same], clothing and personal effects for the duration of the Adventure.

Meals provided [or not] at the sole discretion of the Director, with due regard for availability, season, or any special dietary requirements not disclosed at the outset.

Transport of any remains, in whole or in part, back to the country of Burglar's origin is not included.

...Burglar on a pro-rata basis, but the reverse situation does not apply.

For Company's assumption.

THE CONTRACT DESIGN PROCESS

1 At first, the burglar contract was a simple affair: the text straight from the book, executed in a Dwarven style, but readable by both hobbits and movie audiences. Done. I moved onto my next task.

2 But wait – now we have a film script, which calls for specific wording in the Contract. Okay, no problem, I'll add the appropriate clause … There.

3 What's that? We need more words? Two pages? Alright; scribble scribble…. Still not enough?

4 Let's have more legalese, all sorts of clauses. And let's try some different styles of signatures. Hmmm, this is turning into quite a prop. Done. Again. Maybe …

5 No? We want even MORE? Right. Okay. No half measures now – I'll give them MUCH, MUCH more! Many, many, many more clauses, pages added and appended, various fold-out sections (Alan Lee's idea), tiny writing within tiny writing ('Even tinier!' – Dan Hennah), every available space used, totally baffling to a poor hobbit! This last version took several weeks to compose and write and assemble – and finally, it was approved. Sigh of relief.

Now, Daniel, just in case we accidentally rip it – could you make a backup copy…?

Daniel Reeve, Graphic Artist

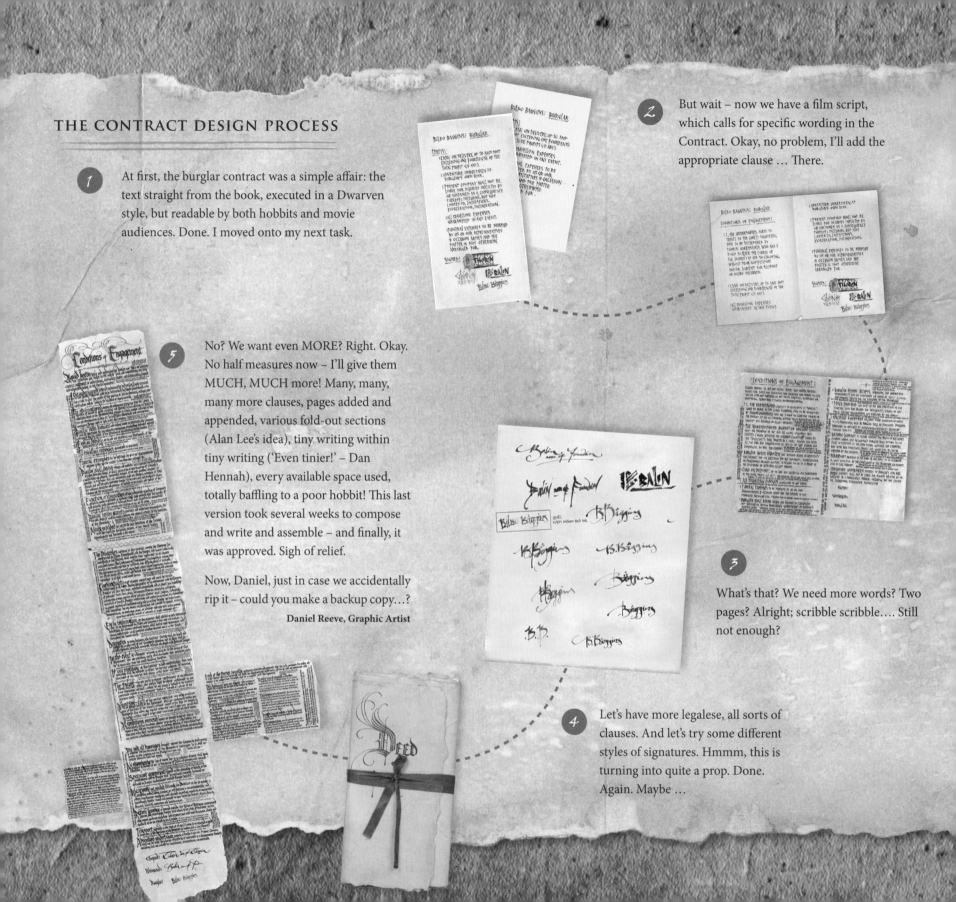